A Study of Juz' One:
Alif Lām Mīm

For the Classroom
Senior Level • General

Arabic Text, Translations,
Explanations & Vocabulary

Compilation: **Abidullah Ghazi**
Ph.D. History of Religion, Harvard University

Translations: **Abdullāh Yūsuf Ali and**
Muhammad Marmaduke Pickthal
Rendered in Modern English

Explanations: **Abdullāh Yūsuf Ali**
Revised and Abridged

IQRA' International Educational Foundation, Chicago

Part of a Comprehensive and Systematic Program of Islamic Studies

A Study of Juz' One: Alif Lām Mīm

First Limited Edition for Review and Opinion

**A Textbook for
Qur'anic Studies
Senior Level / General**

Chief Program Editors
Dr. Abidullah al-Ansari Ghazi
(Ph.D., History of Religion
Harvard University)

Tasneema Khatoon Ghazi
(Ph.D., Curriculum-Reading
University of Minnesota)

Religious Review
Maulana Shu'aib ud-Din Qutub
(Faḍil Dar ul-Ulum, Karachi)

Najiyah Helwani

Language Editing
Hina Naseem Akhtar
(B.S. Zoology, University of Maryland
M.A.T. Pending National Lewis University)

Huda Quraishi-Ahmed
(B.Sc., University of Illinois, Chicago)

English Typesetting
Shaista N. Ali
(M.A. Mass Communications, Karachi
University, Pakistan)

Mahlaqa Patel
(B.Sc., University of Illinois, Chicago)

Arabic Typesetting
Kamal Nazzal
(M.S. Civil Engineering, Moscow)

Cover Design
Kathryn Heimberger
(A.A.S. American Academy of Art)

Printed in USA

Library of Congress Catalog Number 97-72058
ISBN # 1-56316-116-8

IQRA'S NOTE: FOR PARENTS, TEACHERS AND READERS

IQRA' International is pleased to offer *Juz' One: Alif Lām Mīm* as a textbook at the Senior level and as a Qur'ānic reading book for the general public. This publication follows the same organization and methodology used in our now well-established textbooks on the Qur'ān, *Juz' 'Amma: 30*, Part I and II and *Seven Sūrahs*, written at the Junior / General Level. The response to this series has been overwhelming and most Islamic schools immediately including them in their programs of Islamic Studies. IQRA's Qur'ānic Studies Program has also been welcomed by the general public, who is using it to better their understanding of the text of the Qur'ān.

With the publication of *Juz One: Alif Lām Mīm*, we are taking an ambitious step to present the meaning of the entire Qur'ān using this methodology. We shall be publishing, *Insha Allāh*, one *Juz'* every two months and we hope to complete the Qur'ān in five years. This serialization would enable our students and readers to study the Qur'ān in the two major translations of `Abdullah Yusuf `Ali and Muḥammad Marmaduke Pickthall (rendered into modern English) and then follow it word for word. Those students and readers who are following our program of Arabic Studies or use any other program of Arabic would find it extremely helpful and be able to read the Qur'ān directly. Readers will find that most of the words in the text of the Qur'ān repeat themselves and even without a serious effort on their part, they will be able to memorize many Arabic words, know the key Qur'ānic terms and begin to understand the construction of the verses themselves.

We are recommending *Juz '1-4* of this Program (namely: *Juz', One: Alif Lām Mīm: , Juz' Two Sa-Yaqūl, Juz' Three: Tilka Ar-Rusūl and Juz' Four: Lantana Lu Al-Birra*, which cover the study of *Sūrahs Al-Fātiḥah* and *Al-Baqarah, Al 'Imrān and part of An-Nisā'*) for the senior level for grades 9 to 12. These important *Sūrahs* cover all the teachings and major themes of the Qur'ān. A systematic study of these four parts will enable the student to understand and appreciate the Qur'ān fully and follow its vocabulary. Islāmic schools which do not provide Islāmic education up to grade 12 may try to complete at least *Sūrah al-Baqarah* in the Program of Qur'ānic Studies. Students and readers who have studied *Juz' 'Amma 30*, Parts I and II and *Seven Sūrahs* would develop a very good grasp of the meaning and message of the entire Qur'ān.

This series follows the scheme and organization of our earlier textbooks in the Qur'ān series. For the benefit of those students and readers who start with the *Juz' One: Alif Lām Mīm* we wish to explain it once again.

Division of the volume and lesson plan: Each *Rukū'* (section) contains an ***Introduction, Arabic text, two translations*** (`Abdullāh Yūsuf `Ali and M. M. Pickthall), ***Explanation, Important Points to Learn and Reflect Upon, and a complete Vocabulary of Arabic Text***. (Each part of the lesson plan needs some further explanation.)

Transliteration: In transliterating, we followed the Library of Congress system with a few modifications (See Appendix II). We have utilized the phonetic method to facilitate reading. The Arabic definite article *(al)* often assimilates its initial (a) in speech, while in writing, it does appear. Following the phonetic scheme, we have not written it in transliteration within parentheses. A letter appearing in the text but falling silent after the *'Ayah* is also shown in the vocabulary section within parenthesis. In transliterating the *Sūrah,* we have followed only phonetic sound (as it must be pronounced before the *'Ayah*). Before or after the consonant letter of the *'Ayah,* the *ḥarakāt* (*'I'rāb*) do appear in parenthesis but they are not read. For example:

1:1.   *Rabbi al-'ālamīna* is written as *Rabbi-(a)l-'ālamīn(a)* and read as *Rabbi-l-'ālamīn.*

114:1. *Bi-Rabbi an-nāsi* is written as *Bi-Rabbi-(a)n-nās(i)* and read as *Bi-Rabbi-n-nās.*
        Fi Al-Qur'āni al-Karīmi is transliterated as *fi-(a)l-Qur'āni-(a)l-Karīm(i)* and read as *fi-l-Qur'āni-l-Karīm.*

We have followed the phonetic rule in the usage of *Shamsi* (Sun) letters for example:

1:1   *Al-Rahmāni Al-Rahīmi* is transliterated as *Ar-Rahmāni-(a)r-Rahīm(i)* and read as *Ar-Rahmāni-r-Rahīm.*

114:1 *'Ilāhi al-nāsi* is transliterated as *'Ilāhi-(a)n-nās(i)* and read as *Ilāhi-n-nās.*

The entire IQRA' program is designed to teach students reading and understanding of Qur'ānic Arabic. Therefore, we are not including the transliteration of the Qur'ānic text in this series, since we expect the readers to be proficient in reading Arabic by now.

Translations: We have provided two major translations side by side. The first translation is by 'Abdullāh Yūsuf 'Ali, and the second is by Muḥammad Marmaduke Pickthall. A student will greatly benefit in understanding the Qur'ān by these two prominent scholars. Additionally, he/she will also understand the difficulties of translating Arabic text. These original translations in Old English are rendered into modern English without tampering with the text at all. We have also used more accepted Islamic terminology (e.g. Allāh for God, Messenger for Apostle etc.). We have also provided key Arabic terms next to the translation and the meaning of difficult words within parenthesis{ }.

Commentary: For this series, we are using the abbreviated and revised version of the commentary of Abdullah Yūsuf 'Ali and have tried to remain faithful to his understanding of the text. Certain points have been explained further and the compiler has, at some places, added to 'Ali's commentary within parenthesis and his initials {AG}.

Important Points to Learn and Reflect Upon: Each *Rukū'* ends with a section entitled 'Important Points to Learn and Reflect Upon' and recaptures the central passage of the section in three short points.

Glossary Words: The meaning of difficult English words and basic Arabic Qur'ānic terms are provided within parenthesis { } in the text. Therefore, no special glossary of Arabic terms and difficult English words is provided at the end of the lesson or as an appendix.

Vocabulary: The meaning of each word is provided for every *Sūrah* at the end of each section. It will greatly enhance the student's understanding of the Qur'ānic text and will facilitate his/ her in learning of Arabic.

Workbooks: The workbooks, based on the pattern of our familiar *Sīrah Program* and other popular textbooks, are under publication to provide reinforcement, develop educational skills, and allow further practice.

This work is part of IQRA's pioneering efforts to introduce the meaning and message of the Qur'ān at every level to Muslim youth and all other seekers of Truth. We pray to Allāh ﷻ that He accepts this effort and makes it useful to all the lovers of the truth as contained in the final Revelation, the Qur'ān. May this effort bring about a clear understanding of the message of the Qur'ān and the behavior modification that is a natural outcome of Qur'ānic study.

As concerned parents and teachers, we urge you to support this pioneering educational endeavor through your *Du`a'*, advice and participation. We shall appreciate your opinions and comments to help us improve the revised edition.

Chief Editors
7450 Skokie Boulevard,
Skokie, IL. 60077

Jum'ah, 12 Dhu al-Qa`dah 1417H
Friday, 21 March, 1997

SECTION -1-

Sūrah Al-Fātiḥah
1: 1-7
The Opening Chapter / The Opening

INTRODUCTION

Name: This *Sūrah* is named *Al-Fātiḥah* because of its subject matter. *Fātiḥah* is that which opens a book, a subject or any other thing. In other words, *Al-Fātiḥah* is the preface to the Qur'ān. It is also known as the *Umm al-Kitāb,* the "Mother of the Book."

Theme: It is one of the earliest Revelations, and the first complete *Sūrah* to be revealed to Rasūlullāh ﷺ. It is the most important *Sūrah* of the Qur'ān. Rasūlullāh ﷺ said: "Such an important *Sūrah* as this was not sent down to any other prophet." This *Sūrah* is, in fact, a prayer which Allāh ﷻ has provided for all those who wish to approach Him through the *Ṣalāh,* to create a relationship with Him and to receive guidance from His Book, the Qur'ān.

This *Sūrah* creates a strong desire in the heart of the sincere reader to seek guidance and help from Allāh ﷻ, Who alone can grant this guidance. Thus, *Al-Fātiḥah* teaches that the best thing we can do for ourselves is to completely depend upon Allāh ﷻ, the Lord of the Worlds, and the best thing to ask from Him is to seek His guidance to the Straight Path.

This *Sūrah* is recited in each *Rak'ah* (unit) of the ritual prayer.

THE TEXT OF THE QUR'ĀN

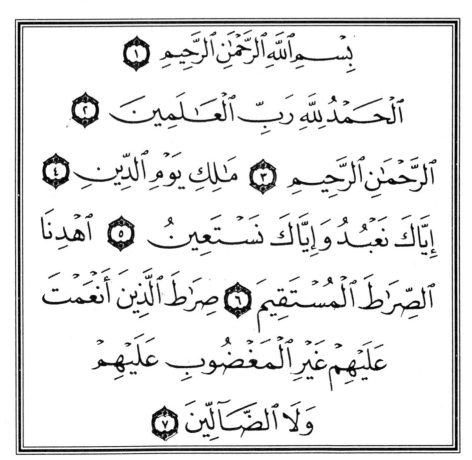

TRANSLATIONS

(A. Y. Ali)

(M. M. Pickthall)

1.   In the name of God, Most Gracious, Most Merciful.

1.   In the name of Allāh, the Beneficent, the Merciful.

2.   Praise be to God, the Cherisher and Sustainer {*Rabb*} of the Worlds:

2.   Praise be to Allāh, Lord of the Worlds:

3.   Most Gracious {*Ar-Raḥmān*} Most Merciful {*Ar-Raḥim*};

3.   The Beneficent, the Merciful:

4.   Master of the Day of Judgment.

4.   Owner of the Day of Judgment.

5.   You do we worship, and Your aid do we seek.

5.   You (alone) we worship; You alone we ask for help.

6.   Show us the straight way {*Aṣ-Ṣirāt Al-Mustaqīm*}

6.   Show us the straight path:

7.   The way of those on whom You have bestowed your Grace, those whose (portion) is not wrath, and who go not astray.

7.   The path of those whom You have favored; Not (the path) of those who earn Your anger nor of those who go astray.

EXPLANATION (A. Y. Ali, Abridged and Revised)

1:   The Arabic words *Raḥmān* and *Raḥim*, translated as "Most Gracious" and "Most Merciful" have their root in the Arabic word *Raḥima*, meaning "to have mercy." Both these words are intensive forms of *Raḥima*, and express the strength and depth of God's Mercy. Mercy may imply kindness, patience, sympathy and forgiveness, all of which a human needs, and which God, the Most Merciful, bestows in abundant measure.

However, there is also a form of Mercy that is always present, even before its need arises. The Grace of Allāh ﷻ is ever-watchful of His creatures, protecting, preserving, guiding, and leading them to clearer light and higher life.

The attribute *ar-Raḥmān* (Most Gracious) cannot be applied to any but God, but the attribute *Raḥim* (Merciful), is a general term, and may also be applied to humans. To remind us of these boundless gifts of God, the formula, *In the name of God, Most Gracious, Most Merciful* is placed at the beginning of every *Sūrah* of the Qur'ān (except the ninth), and is repeated by a Muslim at the beginning of almost every act he undertakes.

2:   The Arabic word *Rabb*, usually translated as Lord, carries the meaning of creating, cherishing, sustaining, bringing to maturity. God cares for all the worlds He has created.

3:   {The two names of Allāh ﷻ *Ar-Raḥmān* and *ar-Raḥim* are once again repeated here, emphasizing how important Divine of Mercy is for us and how Merciful He is. AG}

4:   {On the Day of Judgement, Allāh ﷻ will be the sole Master and Owner. Everyone will be totally dependent on His Mercy and Justice. In this life, He has given us limited freedom to act and a limited ownership of our possessions for a limited period of time. AG}

5:   Once we recognize God's Love, Care, Grace, Mercy, Power and Justice (as Ruler of the Day of Judgement), we must submit to Him completely. We worship Him alone, and ask for His aid only. There is none other worthy of our worship, and none other that will help us.

6:   "Guide us to and in the straight Way." Spiritually, we may be wandering aimlessly. Thus, the first step is to find the Way. The second step is to remain steadfast in the Way. When our own wisdom may fail, we must ask for Allāh's ﷻ guidance. With a little spiritual insight, we will be able to differentiate between those people who walk in the light of Allāh's ﷻ Grace, and those who walk in the darkness of His Wrath. {The Qur'ān, "the book that is a guidance to the righteous," *(al-Baqarah 2:2)* itself was sent as an answer to this prayer. The *Sunnah* of Rasūlullāh ﷺ demonstrates how to walk steadily on that Way. AG}

7:   The Wrath (al-Ghaḍab) is the opposite of Grace, Peace and Harmony (al-In'ām). Note that our own actions are responsible for falling from His Grace and inviting His Wrath. Apparently, there are two kinds of people deserving Wrath (al-Maghḍūb): those who choose to be in the darkness of Wrath through their own evil actions, and those who go astray out of ignorance. The first kind are those who deliberately break God's law; the second are those who stray out of carelessness or negligence. Both are responsible for their own acts or omissions. {The first kind do not receive guidance, and their hearts are sealed from receiving any Light (al-Baqarah 2:6-7). The second kind have a chance to come back to guidance, if they repent. For such people, the Qur'ān and the *Sunnah* of Rasūlullāh ﷺ await to guide them, and Allāh's ﷻ Grace awaits to forgive and accept them. AG} In contrast to both of these kinds of people are the righteous people, who have chosen to be in the light of God's Grace. His Grace not only protects them from wrongdoing (as they have already submitted their will to Him) but continuously guides them to the Way of the blessed.

IMPORTANT POINTS TO LEARN AND REFLECT UPON

- Allāh ﷻ is Most Gracious and Most Merciful.

- We should worship Him alone and ask only His help in all matters.

- We must pray to Him ﷻ to give us guidance and keep us on straight path.

ARABIC GLOSSARY WORDS

بِسْمِ اللهِ الرَّحْمٰنِ الرَّحِيمِ

(1) بِسْمِ اللهِ	In the name of Allah	وَ إِيَّاكَ	and You (alone)
الرَّحْمٰنِ	the Compassionate	نَسْتَعِينُ	we ask for help
الرَّحِيمِ	the Merciful	(6) اهْدِنَا	guide us
(2) اَلْحَمْدُ	All praise	الصِّرَاطَ	to the path
للهِ	is for Allah	اَلْمُسْتَقِيمَ	(that is) straight
رَبِّ	the Lord of	(7) صِرَاطَ	Path of
اَلْعٰلَمِينَ	the worlds	اَلَّذِينَ	those whom
(3) اَلرَّحْمٰنِ	The Compassionate	أَنْعَمْتَ	You blessed
الرَّحِيمِ	The Merciful	عَلَيْهِمْ	upon them
(4) مٰلِكِ	Master of	غَيْرِ الْمَغْضُوبِ	not (the path of) those Your
يَوْمِ الدِّينِ	the Day of Judgment		wrath was brought down
(5) إِيَّاكَ	You (alone)	عَلَيْهِمْ	upon them
نَعْبُدُ	we worship	وَ لَا الضَّالِّينَ	nor those who go astray

SECTION -1-

Sūrah Al-Baqarah
2: 1-7

INTRODUCTION

Name: The name *Al-Baqarah* is derived from the Story of the Sacrifice of the Cow (2:67-71). Although the subject matter of this *Sūrah* is much broader than this specific story, its moral is a central theme of this *Sūrah*. Allāh ﷻ asked for the sacrifice of a cow from the Israelites as atonement for their sins. The Israelites were reluctant to obey the order of Allāh ﷻ and came up with all kinds of excuses. Finally, they did perform the sacrifice, but in the eyes of Allāh ﷻ, they did not. The moral of the story is:

- When Allāh ﷻ asks us to do something, we must do it with pleasure.

- When a clear command is issued by Allāh ﷻ, we must never come up with excuses, however genuine they may sound to us,

- If we obey the orders of Allāh ﷻ reluctantly, our obedience is meaningless to Him.

- Any act of worship lacking sincerity is rejected by Allāh ﷻ and is not counted in the *Ākhirah*, the Hereafter.

Just as *Sūrah Al-Fātiḥah* (The Opening) sums up the essence of the Qur'ān in seven beautiful verses, this *Sūrah* sums up in 286 verses the entire teachings of the Qur'ān.

Theme: It begins by classifying humans into the three broad categories (verses -2-19), depending on how they receive and respond to Allāh's ﷻ message.

This leads to the story of the creation of the first human being, Ādam ﷺ, the high destiny intended for him, his fall, and hope of salvation given to him (2:30-39).

Israel's story {as the first believing community, preceding Christians and Muslims. AG} is then told, according to their own records and traditions: what privileges they received and how they behaved (2:40-86). Through this story, the Qur'ān again illustrates the general principle of the rise and fall of nations {for the benefit of the Muslim community. AG}.

Reference is made to Mūsa ﷺ and Isā ﷺ and their struggles with an unruly people. It shows how the People of the Book falsely played their own lights and rejected Final revelation and the last Messenger in their pride (2:87-121).

They falsely laid exclusive claim to the heritage of Father Ibrāhim ﷺ. He was indeed a righteous *'Imām* (leader); he was the ancestor of Ismā`il 's line (Arabs) as well as of Isḥāq's Israeli line (the Jews). But most important of all, he was the spiritual father of all the *Ḥanif* (those who are righteous and submit to Allāh ﷻ alone). He, with his eldest son Ismā`il ﷺ, built the Ka'bah and purified it, thus establishing the first and most ancient house of worship of Allāh ﷻ (2:122-141).

The Ka'bah was now to be the center of universal worship and the symbol of Allāh's ﷻ universal message: al-Islam (2:142-167).

The Islamic *'Ummah* (brotherhood) having thus been established, ordinances are laid down for the social life of the community, with the teachings (2:177) that righteousness does not consist in formalities, but in faith, kindness, prayer, charity, righteousness, and patience under suffering. The ordinances relate to drink, bequests, fasts, *jihād*, wine and gambling, treatment of orphans and women, etc. (2:168-242).

In case the subject of *jihād* should be misunderstood, it is taken up again in the story of Saul (Talūt), Goliath (Jalūt) and David (Da'ūd), in contrast of the story of Jesus (`Isā) (2:243-253).

And so the lesson is enforced that true virtue lies in practical deeds of courage, kindness, and good faith (2:254-283), and Allāh's ﷻ nature is called to mind in the sublime `Āyat al-Kursi, the "Verse of the Throne" (2:255).

The *Sūrah* ends with an appeal to faith, obedience, personal responsibility, and prayer (2:284-286).

This is the longest *Surah* of the Qur'ān, and in it occurs the longest verse (2:282). The name of the *Surah* is from the Parable of the Cow in 2:67-71. The story shows the uselessness of insincere obedience. When faith is lost, even when at last they obey in the letter, they fail in the spirit.

THE TEXT OF THE QUR'ĀN

بِسْمِ اللَّهِ الرَّحْمَٰنِ الرَّحِيمِ

الٓمٓ ۝ ذَٰلِكَ الْكِتَٰبُ لَا رَيْبَ ۛ فِيهِ ۛ هُدًى لِّلْمُتَّقِينَ ۝ الَّذِينَ يُؤْمِنُونَ بِالْغَيْبِ وَيُقِيمُونَ الصَّلَوٰةَ وَمِمَّا رَزَقْنَٰهُمْ يُنفِقُونَ ۝ وَالَّذِينَ يُؤْمِنُونَ بِمَا أُنزِلَ إِلَيْكَ وَمَا أُنزِلَ مِن قَبْلِكَ وَبِالْآخِرَةِ هُمْ يُوقِنُونَ ۝ أُولَٰئِكَ عَلَىٰ هُدًى مِّن رَّبِّهِمْ ۖ وَأُولَٰئِكَ هُمُ الْمُفْلِحُونَ ۝ إِنَّ الَّذِينَ كَفَرُوا سَوَاءٌ عَلَيْهِمْ ءَأَنذَرْتَهُمْ أَمْ لَمْ تُنذِرْهُمْ لَا يُؤْمِنُونَ ۝ خَتَمَ اللَّهُ عَلَىٰ قُلُوبِهِمْ وَعَلَىٰ سَمْعِهِمْ ۖ وَعَلَىٰ أَبْصَٰرِهِمْ غِشَٰوَةٌ ۖ وَلَهُمْ عَذَابٌ عَظِيمٌ ۝

TRANSLATIONS

Section 1: 1-7 (A. Y. Ali)

1. A. L. M.
2. This is the Book {*Kitab: holy book*}; in it is guidance {*Huda*} sure, without doubt, to those who fear Allāh - {*al-Muttaqīn: who have Taqwā*}
3. Who believe in the Unseen {*Al-Ghaib*} are steadfast in prayer, and spend out of what We have provided for them;
4. And who believe in the Revelation sent to you, and sent before your time, and (in their hearts) have the assurance of the Hereafter {*Ākhirah*}
5. They are on (true) guidance {*Huda*} from their Lord, and it is these who will prosper {*Al-Muflihūn*}
6. As to those who reject Faith, it is the same to them whether you warn them or do not warn them; they will not believe.
7. Allāh has set a seal {*Khatam*} on their hearts and on their hearing, and on their eyes is a veil; great is the penalty they (incur).

Section 1: 1-7 (M. M. Pickthall)

1. Alif. Lām. Mīm.
2. This is the Scripture whereof there is no doubt, a guidance unto those who ward off.
3. Who believe in the unseen and establish worship, and spend of that We have bestowed upon them;
4. And who believe in that which is revealed unto You (Muḥammad) and that which was revealed before you, and are certain of the Hereafter.
5. These depend on guidance from their Lord. These are the successful.
6. As for the disbelievers, whether you warn them or you warn them not it is all one for them; they believe not.
7. Allāh has sealed their hearing and their hearts, and on their eyes there is a covering. Theirs will be an awful doom.

EXPLANATION

1: These are abbreviated letters on which a general discussion will be found in Appendix I at the end of this *Juz'*.

2: *Taqwā* and the verbs and nouns {*al-Muttaqi*: plural *al Muttaqīn*} connected with the root, have a variety of meanings in English: (1) the fear of God (2) restraint, or guarding one's tongue, hand, and heart from evil; (3) hence righteousness, piety and good conduct. All these ideas are implied in the translation, and one or another of them can be indicated according to the context. See also *Muḥammad* 47: 17 and *Al-Muddaththir* 74:56, note.

3: All bounties come from God. They may be physical gifts, e.g. food, wealth, etc.; intangible gifts, e.g. influence, power, talents, etc.; or spiritual gifts, e.g., insight into good and evil and understanding of human nature. We are to use all in humility and moderation. But we are also to give out of every one of them something that contributes to the well-being of others.

4: Righteousness (*Taqwā*) comes from a secure faith, from sincere devotion to God, and from unselfish service to humanity.

5: Prosperity must be taken as referring to all the kinds of blessings which we discussed in the note to 2:3 above. The proper use of one kind leads to an increase in that and other kinds, and that is prosperity.

6: *Kafara, kufr, kafr*, and derivative forms of the word (*Kāfir*; plural *Kuffār*: one who rejects faith), imply a deliberate rejection of faith as opposed to a mistaken idea of God or faith. A mistaken idea is not inconsistent with an earnest desire to see the truth. Where there is such desire, by this Grace and Mercy, God gives guidance. But that guidance is not available when it is deliberately rejected. The possibility of rejection follows from God's grant of free will to humans.

7: All actions are referred to God. Therefore, when we get the penalty of our deliberate sin, the penalty is meted out according to the justice of God. The penalty here is the opposite of the prosperity referred to in note 5.

IMPORTANT POINTS TO LEARN AND REFLECT UPON

- The Qur'ān is a book of guidance for those who have *Taqwā*.

- Those who have *Taqwā* receive guidance from Allāh ﷻ and are successful.

- Those who reject faith and do *Kufr* Allāh ﷻ seals their hearts from receiving guidance.

ARABIC GLOSSARY WORDS

بِسْمِ اللهِ الرَّحْمٰنِ الرَّحِيمِ

(1) اَلٓمَّ	(Letters) *Alif, Lam, Mim*	أُنْزِلَ	sent down
(2) ذٰلِكَ	That (is)	إِلَيْكَ	to you
الْكِتٰبُ	the Book	وَمَآ	and what
لَا	(there is) no	أُنْزِلَ	was sent down
رَيْبَ	doubt	مِنْ قَبْلِكَ	before you
فِيهِ	in it	وَ بِالْاٰخِرَةِ	and in the Hereafter
هُدًى	guidance	هُمْ	they
لِّلْمُتَّقِينَ	those who fear (Allah)	يُوقِنُونَ	believe with certainty
(3) اَلَّذِينَ	Those who	(5) أُولٰئِكَ	Those are
يُؤْمِنُونَ	believe	عَلَى	on
بِالْغَيْبِ	in the Hidden, Unseen	هُدًى	guidance
وَ يُقِيمُونَ	and (who) establish	مِّنْ	from
الصَّلٰوةَ	the prayer, the worship	رَّبِّهِمْ	their Lord
وَمِمَّا	and from what	وَ أُلٰئِكَ	and those are
رَزَقْنٰهُمْ	We provided them	هُمُ	they (alone) are
يُنْفِقُونَ	they spend	الْمُفْلِحُونَ	the successful
(4) وَ الَّذِينَ	And those who	(6) إِنَّ	Indeed
يُؤْمِنُونَ	believe	اَلَّذِينَ	those who
بِمَآ	in what	كَفَرُوا	denied

سَوَآءٌ	it is all the same		قُلُوبِهِمْ	their hearts
عَلَيْهِمْ	on them		وَعَلَىٰ	and upon
ءَأَنْذَرْتَهُمْ	whether you warn them		سَمْعِهِمْ	their (sense of) hearing
أَمْ	or		وَعَلَىٰٓ	and on
لَمْ	do not		أَبْصَارِهِمْ	their eyes (perception)
تُنْذِرْهُمْ	warn them		غِشَاوَةٌ	(there is) a covering
لَا يُؤْمِنُونَ	they shall not believe		وَّ لَهُمْ	and for them
خَتَمَ اللهُ (7)	Allah sealed		عَذَابٌ	there is punishment
عَلَىٰ	upon		عَظِيمٌ	great

SECTION -2-

Sūrah Al-Baqarah
2: 8-20

THE TEXT OF THE QUR'ĀN

بِسْمِ اللَّهِ الرَّحْمَٰنِ الرَّحِيمِ

وَمِنَ النَّاسِ

مَن يَقُولُ ءَامَنَّا بِاللَّهِ وَبِالْيَوْمِ الْأَخِرِ وَمَا هُم بِمُؤْمِنِينَ ﴿٨﴾

يُخَٰدِعُونَ اللَّهَ وَالَّذِينَ ءَامَنُوا وَمَا يَخْدَعُونَ إِلَّا أَنفُسَهُمْ

وَمَا يَشْعُرُونَ ﴿٩﴾ فِي قُلُوبِهِم مَّرَضٌ فَزَادَهُمُ اللَّهُ مَرَضًا

وَلَهُمْ عَذَابٌ أَلِيمٌ بِمَا كَانُوا يَكْذِبُونَ ﴿١٠﴾ وَإِذَا قِيلَ لَهُمْ

لَا تُفْسِدُوا فِي الْأَرْضِ قَالُوا إِنَّمَا نَحْنُ مُصْلِحُونَ ﴿١١﴾

أَلَا إِنَّهُمْ هُمُ الْمُفْسِدُونَ وَلَٰكِن لَّا يَشْعُرُونَ ﴿١٢﴾ وَإِذَا قِيلَ

لَهُمْ ءَامِنُوا كَمَا ءَامَنَ النَّاسُ قَالُوا أَنُؤْمِنُ كَمَا ءَامَنَ السُّفَهَاءُ

أَلَا إِنَّهُمْ هُمُ السُّفَهَاءُ وَلَٰكِن لَّا يَعْلَمُونَ ﴿١٣﴾ وَإِذَا لَقُوا

الَّذِينَ ءَامَنُوا قَالُوا ءَامَنَّا وَإِذَا خَلَوْا إِلَىٰ شَيَٰطِينِهِمْ قَالُوا إِنَّا

مَعَكُمْ إِنَّمَا نَحْنُ مُسْتَهْزِءُونَ ﴿١٤﴾ اللَّهُ يَسْتَهْزِئُ بِهِمْ وَيَمُدُّهُمْ

فِي طُغْيَٰنِهِمْ يَعْمَهُونَ ﴿١٥﴾ أُولَٰئِكَ الَّذِينَ اشْتَرَوُا الضَّلَٰلَةَ

بِالْهُدَىٰ فَمَا رَبِحَت تِّجَٰرَتُهُمْ وَمَا كَانُوا مُهْتَدِينَ ﴿١٦﴾

مَثَلُهُمْ كَمَثَلِ ٱلَّذِى ٱسْتَوْقَدَ نَارًا فَلَمَّا أَضَآءَتْ مَا حَوْلَهُۥ

ذَهَبَ ٱللَّهُ بِنُورِهِمْ وَتَرَكَهُمْ فِى ظُلُمَٰتٍ لَّا يُبْصِرُونَ ﴿١٧﴾ صُمٌّ

بُكْمٌ عُمْىٌ فَهُمْ لَا يَرْجِعُونَ ﴿١٨﴾ أَوْ كَصَيِّبٍ مِّنَ ٱلسَّمَآءِ فِيهِ

ظُلُمَٰتٌ وَرَعْدٌ وَبَرْقٌ يَجْعَلُونَ أَصَٰبِعَهُمْ فِىٓ ءَاذَانِهِم مِّنَ ٱلصَّوَٰعِقِ

حَذَرَ ٱلْمَوْتِ وَٱللَّهُ مُحِيطٌ بِٱلْكَٰفِرِينَ ﴿١٩﴾ يَكَادُ ٱلْبَرْقُ يَخْطَفُ

أَبْصَٰرَهُمْ كُلَّمَآ أَضَآءَ لَهُم مَّشَوْاْ فِيهِ وَإِذَآ أَظْلَمَ عَلَيْهِمْ قَامُواْ

وَلَوْ شَآءَ ٱللَّهُ لَذَهَبَ بِسَمْعِهِمْ وَأَبْصَٰرِهِمْ إِنَّ ٱللَّهَ عَلَىٰ كُلِّ

شَىْءٍ قَدِيرٌ ﴿٢٠﴾

TRANSLATIONS

Section 2: 8-20 (A. Y. Ali)

8.   Of the people, there are some who say: "We believe in Allāh and the Last Day;" but they do not (really) believe.

9.   Fain would they deceive Allāh and those who believe, but they only deceive themselves, and realize (it) not!

10.   In their hearts is a disease; and Allāh has increased their disease: and grievous is the penalty they (incur) because they are false (to themselves).

11.   When it is said to them: "Make not mischief on the earth," they say: "Why, we only want to make peace!" {Muṣliḥūn}

12.   Of a surety, they are the ones who make mischief {Mufsidūn} but they realize (it) not.

13.   When it is said to them: "Believe as the others believe:" they say: "Shall we be-

Section 2: 8-20 (M. M. Pickthall)

8.   And of mankind are some who say: We believe in Allāh and the Last Day, when they believe not.

9.   They think to beguile {deceive} Allah and those who believe, and they beguile none save themselves; but they perceive not.

10.   In their hearts is a disease, and Allāh increases their disease. A painful doom is theirs because they lie.

11.   And when it is said unto them: Make not mischief in the earth, they say: We are peacemakers only.

12.   Are not they indeed the mischief makers? But they perceive not.

13.   And when it is said unto them: Believe as the people believe, they say: Shall we

lieve as the fools believe?" Nay, of a surety they are the fools, but they do not know.

believe as the foolish believe? Are not they indeed the foolish? But they know not.

14. When they meet those who believe, they say: "We believe;" but when they are alone with their evil ones {*shayāṭin*} they say: "We are really with you we (were) only jesting."

14. And when they fall in with those who believe, they say: We believe; but when they go apart to their devils they declare: Lo! We are with you; verily, we did but mock.

15. Allāh will throw back their mockery on them, and give them rope in their trespasses {*Tughyān: sins, offenses*}; so they will wander like blind ones (to and fro).

15. Allāh (Himself) does mock them, leaving them to wander blindly on in their contumacy {defiance}.

16. These are they who have bartered {traded} guidance for error {*Dalāl*} but their traffic {trade} is profitless, and they have lost true direction {*Muhtadān: guided ones*}

16. These are they who purchase error at the price of guidance, so their commerce does not prosper, neither are they guided.

17. Their similitude {example} is that of a man who kindled a fire; when it lighted all around him, Allāh took away their light and left them in utter darkness, so they not see.

17. Their likeness is as the likeness of one who kindles fire, and when it sheds its light around him Allāh takes away their light and leaves them in darkness, where they cannot see,

18. Deaf, dumb, and blind, they will not return (to the path).

18. Deaf, dumb and blind; and they return not

19. Or (another similitude) is that of a rain-laden cloud from the sky; in it are zones of darkness, and thunder and lightning: they press their fingers in their ears to keep out the stunning thunderclap, the while they are in terror of death. But Allāh is ever round the rejectors of Faith {*Kāfirin*}!

19. Or like a rainstorm from the sky, wherein is darkness, thunder and the flash of lightning. They thrust their fingers in their ears by reason of the thunderclaps, for fear of death. Allāh encompasses the disbelievers (in His guidance).

20. The lightning all but snatches away their sight; every time the light (helps) them, they walk therein, and when the darkness grows on them, they stand still, and if Allāh willed, He could take away their faculty of hearing and seeing; for Allāh has power over all things {*Qadīr*}

20. The lightning almost snatches away their sight from them. As often as it flashes forth for them they walk therein, and when it darkens against them, they stand still. If Allāh willed, He could destroy their hearing and their sight. Lo! Allāh is Able to do all things.

EXPLANATION

8: We now come to a third category of people, the *Munāfiqūn* or Hypocrites. They are untrue to themselves, and therefore, their hearts are diseased (2:10). They are curable, but if they harden their hearts, they soon pass into the category of those who deliberately reject the light.

9: {They readily tell lies about their faith to deceive the Muslims and Allāh ﷻ. God knew these people. Prophet Muḥammad ﷺ and his believers also recognized them through their duplicity. Such people still exist today, of course. They think they are smart, but in fact, they are committing an act of great folly without realizing it. AG}

10: The insincere person, who thinks he can get the best of both worlds by compromising with good and evil, only increases the disease of his heart, because he is not true to himself.

11-12: Much mischief is caused (sometimes unwittingly) by people who think that they have a mission of peace, when they have not even a true perception of right and wrong.

13: This is another face of the Hypocrite. "Faith," he says, "is good enough for fools." But his rejection may be the greatest folly in the eyes of God.

14: A deeper phase of insincerity is actual duplicity, but it never pays in the end. If we compare such a person to a trader, he ultimately loses in the bargain.

15-16: {Allāh Himself increases them in their obstinacy because of their evil deeds. As they have closed the doors of guidance upon themselves, Allāh helps them to do so. Their trade of evil for good will not benefit them in the end.}

17-18: The man wanted light; he only kindled a fire. It produced a blaze and won the applause of all around. But, it did not last long. When the flame went out, as was inevitable, the darkness was worse than before, and they all lost their way. In the confusion, they could not speak, hear or see each other, so they ended up like the rejectors of Faith (2:7), dumb, deaf and blind.

19-20: A graphic simile applying to those who reject Faith. In their pride, they are normally undisturbed. But, what happens when a great storm breaks over them? They cover their ears against the thunderclaps, and the lightning nearly blinds them. In the intervals of deafening noise and blinding flashes, when there are moments of steady light, these people take advantage of them; but as the light disappears, they are plunged into darkness.

IMPORTANT POINTS TO LEARN AND REFLECT UPON

- The *Munāfiqūn*, the Hypocrites say they believe, but, in fact, they do not believe.

- The *Munāfiqūn* think they are deceiving Allāh and the believers but, in fact, they are deceiving themselves.

- Allāh has power over everything, but he has given a chance to the *Munāfiqūn*, in case they return to the truth.

ARABIC GLOSSARY WORDS

بِسْمِ اللهِ الرَّحْمٰنِ الرَّحِيمِ

(8) وَمِنَ	And among	وَ الَّذِينَ	and those
النَّاس	the people	اٰمَنُوا	who believed
مَنْ يَقُولُ	(there are a type of people) who say	وَمَا يَخْدَعُونَ	and they do not deceive
اٰمَنَّا	we believed	إِلَّا	except
بِاللهِ	in Allah	أَنْفُسَهُمْ	themselves
وَبِالْيَوْمِ الْأٰخِرِ	and in the Last Day	وَمَا يَشْعُرُونَ	and they do not perceive
وَمَاهُمْ	and they are not	(10) فِي قُلُوبِهِمْ	In their hearts (there is)
بِمُؤْمِنِينَ	believers	مَرَضٌ	a disease
(9) يُخَادِعُونَ	They deceive (aim at deceiving)	فَزَادَهُمُ اللَّهُ	so Allah increased (for) them
اللَّهَ	Allah	مَرَضًا	disease

وَّ لَهُمْ	and for them	أَلَا	beware
عَذَابٌ	(there is) punishment	إِنَّهُمْ	indeed they
أَلِيمٌ	painful	هُمُ	they themselves
بِمَا	because of	الَسُّفَهَاءُ	are the foolish ones
كَانُوا يَكْذِبُونَ	their lying (lit. they were lying)	وَ لَٰكِن	and yet
(11) وَ إِذَا	And when	لَا يَعْلَمُونَ	they do not know
قِيلَ	it is said	(14) وَ إِذَا	And when
لَهُمْ	to them	لَقُوا	they meet (with)
لَا تُفْسِدُوا	do not corrupt	الَّذِينَ	those who
فِى الْأَرْضِ	in the land	اٰمَنُوا	believe
قَالُوا	they say	قَالُوا	they say
إِنَّمَا نَحْنُ	in fact, we are only	اٰمَنَّا	we believe
مُصْلِحُونَ	reformers	وَ إِذَا	and when
(12) أَلَا	Beware	خَلَوْا	they are alone
إِنَّهُمْ هُمُ	indeed they, they (alone) are		(i.e. have their private meeting)
الَمُفْسِدُونَ	the corrupt ones	إِلَى شَيَاطِينِهِمْ	with their satans
وَ لَٰكِنْ	and yet	قَالُوا	they say
لَا يَشْعُرُونَ	they do not perceive	إِنَّا	verily we
(13) وَ إِذَا	And when	مَعَكُمْ	are with you
قِيلَ	it is said	إِنَّمَا	only
لَهُمْ	to them	نَحْنُ	we
اٰمِنُوا	believe	مُسْتَهْزِءُونَ	(are) mocking (lit. are mockers)
كَمَا	just as	(15) اَللَّهُ يَسْتَهْزِئُ	Allah mocks
اٰمَنَ	believed	بِهِمْ	with them
الَنَّاسُ	the people	وَ يَمُدُّهُمْ	and extends them
قَالُوا	they say	فِى	in
أَنُؤْمِنُ	should we believe?	طُغْيَانِهِمْ	their transgression
كَمَا اٰمَنَ	just as believed	يَعْمَهُونَ	they wander blindly
الَسُّفَهَاءُ	the foolish ones	(16) أُولَٰئِكَ الَّذِينَ	Those are the ones who

اِشْتَرَوُا	bought	ظُلُمٰتٌ	darkness (lit. darknesses)
اَلضَّلٰلَةَ	the misguidance	وَّ رَعْدٌ	and thunder
بِالْهُدٰى	with the guidance	وَّ بَرْقٌ	and lightning
فَمَا رَبِحَت	so made no profit	يَجْعَلُوْنَ	they put
تِجَارَتُهُمْ	their trade	أَصَابِعَهُمْ	their fingers
وَمَا كَانُوا	and they were not	فِى	into
مُهْتَدِيْنَ	guided ones	اٰذَانِهِمْ	their ears
(17) مَثَلُهُمْ	Their example is	مِنَ	from (due to)
كَمَثَلِ	like the example of	اَلصَّوَاعِقِ	the thunderclaps
الَّذِى	the one who	حَذَرَ	fearing (lit. being cautious of)
اسْتَوْقَدَ	lighted up	اَلْمَوْتِ	the death
نَارًا	a fire	وَ اللهُ	and Allah
فَلَمَّآ	so when	مُحِيْطٌ	is encompassing
أَضَآءَتْ	it lighted	بِالْكٰفِرِيْنَ	the disbelievers
مَاحَوْلَهُ	his surrounding	(20) يَكَادُ	(It) is near that
ذَهَبَ اللهُ	Allah took away	اَلْبَرْقُ	the lightning
بِنُوْرِهِمْ	their light	يَخْطَفُ	snatches
وَ تَرَكَهُمْ	and He left them	أَبْصَارَهُمْ	their eyes
فِى ظُلُمٰتٍ	in darkness (lit. darknesses)	كُلَّمَآ	whenever
لَا يُبْصِرُوْنَ	they do not see	أَضَآءَ	it lights
(18) صُمٌّ	They are deaf	لَهُمْ	for them
بُكْمٌ	dumb	مَّشَوْا فِيْهِ	they walk in it
عُمْىٌ	blind	وَ إِذَآ	and when
فَهُمْ	so they	أَظْلَمَ	it darkens
لَا يَرْجِعُوْنَ	would not return	عَلَيْهِمْ	on them
(19) أَوْ	Or (their situation is that of)	قَامُوْا	they stand
كَصَيِّبٍ	heavy rain	وَ لَوْ	and if
مِّنَ السَّمَآءِ	from the sky	شَآءَ اللهُ	Allah had (so) wanted (willed)
فِيْهِ	in it (there is)	لَذَهَبَ	He would have taken away

بِسَمْعِهِمْ	their hearing	عَلٰى كُلِّ شَىْءٍ	on everything
وَ أَبْصَارِهِمْ	and their eyes (sight)	قَدِيرٌ	Powerful
إِنَّ اللهَ	indeed Allah is		

SECTION -3-

Sūrah Al-Baqarah
2: 21-29

THE TEXT OF THE QUR'ĀN

بِسْمِ اللّٰهِ الرَّحْمٰنِ الرَّحِيمِ

يَا أَيُّهَا النَّاسُ اعْبُدُوا رَبَّكُمُ الَّذِي خَلَقَكُمْ وَالَّذِينَ مِن قَبْلِكُمْ لَعَلَّكُمْ تَتَّقُونَ ۞ الَّذِي جَعَلَ لَكُمُ الْأَرْضَ فِرَاشًا وَالسَّمَاءَ بِنَاءً وَأَنزَلَ مِنَ السَّمَاءِ مَاءً فَأَخْرَجَ بِهِ مِنَ الثَّمَرَاتِ رِزْقًا لَّكُمْ فَلَا تَجْعَلُوا لِلَّهِ أَندَادًا وَأَنتُمْ تَعْلَمُونَ ۞ وَإِن كُنتُمْ فِي رَيْبٍ مِّمَّا نَزَّلْنَا عَلَىٰ عَبْدِنَا فَأْتُوا بِسُورَةٍ مِّن مِّثْلِهِ وَادْعُوا شُهَدَاءَكُم مِّن دُونِ اللّٰهِ إِن كُنتُمْ صَادِقِينَ ۞ فَإِن لَّمْ تَفْعَلُوا وَلَن تَفْعَلُوا فَاتَّقُوا النَّارَ الَّتِي وَقُودُهَا النَّاسُ وَالْحِجَارَةُ أُعِدَّتْ لِلْكَافِرِينَ ۞ وَبَشِّرِ الَّذِينَ آمَنُوا وَعَمِلُوا الصَّالِحَاتِ أَنَّ لَهُمْ جَنَّاتٍ تَجْرِي مِن تَحْتِهَا الْأَنْهَارُ كُلَّمَا رُزِقُوا مِنْهَا مِن ثَمَرَةٍ رِّزْقًا قَالُوا هَٰذَا الَّذِي رُزِقْنَا مِن قَبْلُ وَأُتُوا بِهِ مُتَشَابِهًا وَلَهُمْ فِيهَا أَزْوَاجٌ مُّطَهَّرَةٌ وَهُمْ فِيهَا خَالِدُونَ ۞ ۞ إِنَّ اللّٰهَ لَا يَسْتَحْيِي أَن يَضْرِبَ مَثَلًا مَّا بَعُوضَةً فَمَا

فَوْقَهَا ۚ فَأَمَّا ٱلَّذِينَ ءَامَنُوا فَيَعْلَمُونَ أَنَّهُ ٱلْحَقُّ مِن رَّبِّهِمْ ۖ وَأَمَّا ٱلَّذِينَ كَفَرُوا فَيَقُولُونَ مَاذَآ أَرَادَ ٱللَّهُ بِهَٰذَا مَثَلًا ۘ يُضِلُّ بِهِۦ كَثِيرًا وَيَهْدِى بِهِۦ كَثِيرًا ۚ وَمَا يُضِلُّ بِهِۦٓ إِلَّا ٱلْفَٰسِقِينَ ﴿٢٦﴾ ٱلَّذِينَ يَنقُضُونَ عَهْدَ ٱللَّهِ مِنۢ بَعْدِ مِيثَٰقِهِۦ وَيَقْطَعُونَ مَآ أَمَرَ ٱللَّهُ بِهِۦٓ أَن يُوصَلَ وَيُفْسِدُونَ فِى ٱلْأَرْضِ ۚ أُو۟لَٰٓئِكَ هُمُ ٱلْخَٰسِرُونَ ﴿٢٧﴾ كَيْفَ تَكْفُرُونَ بِٱللَّهِ وَكُنتُمْ أَمْوَٰتًا فَأَحْيَٰكُمْ ۖ ثُمَّ يُمِيتُكُمْ ثُمَّ يُحْيِيكُمْ ثُمَّ إِلَيْهِ تُرْجَعُونَ ﴿٢٨﴾ هُوَ ٱلَّذِى خَلَقَ لَكُم مَّا فِى ٱلْأَرْضِ جَمِيعًا ثُمَّ ٱسْتَوَىٰٓ إِلَى ٱلسَّمَآءِ فَسَوَّىٰهُنَّ سَبْعَ سَمَٰوَٰتٍ ۚ وَهُوَ بِكُلِّ شَىْءٍ عَلِيمٌ ﴿٢٩﴾

TRANSLATIONS

Section 3: 21-29 (A. Y. Ali)

21.   O you people! Adore your Guardian Lord {*Rabb*} who created you and those who came before you, that you may have the chance to learn righteousness {*Taqwā*}

22.   Who has made the earth your couch and the heavens your canopy {shelter}; and sent down rain from the heavens; and brought forth therewith fruits for your sustenance; then set not up rivals unto Allāh when you know (the truth).

23.   And if you are in doubt as to what We have revealed from time to time to Our servant, then produce a *Surah* like thereunto;

Section 3: 21-29 (M. M. Pickthall)

21.   O mankind! Worship your Lord, Who has created you and those before you, so that you may ward off (evil).

22.   Who has appointed the earth a resting-place for you, and the sky a canopy; and causes water to pour down from the sky, thereby producing fruits as food for you. And do not set up rivals to Allāh when ye know (better).

23.   And if you are in doubt concerning that which We reveal unto Our slave (Muḥammad), then produce a *Surah* or the

and call your witnesses or helpers (if there are any) besides Allāh, if your (doubts) are true {*Sadiqīn*}.

like thereof, and call your witnesses beside Allāh if you are truthful.

24. But if you cannot - and of a surety you cannot - then fear the Fire whose fuel is men and stones - which is prepared for those who reject Faith {*Kāfirīn*}.

24. And if you do it not, and you can never do it - then guard yourselves against the Fire prepared for disbelievers, whose fuel is of men and stones.

25. But give glad tidings to those who believe and work righteousness {*Salihāt*}, that their portion is Gardens {*Jannāt*} beneath which rivers flow. Every time they are fed with fruits therefrom, they say: "Why, this is what we were fed with before," for they are given things in similitude; and they have therein companions pure (and holy) {*Mutahharah*}; and they abide therein (forever).

25. And give glad tidings (O Muhammad) unto those who believe and do good works; that theirs are Gardens underneath which rivers flow; as often as they are regaled with food of the fruit thereof, they say: This is what was given us aforetime {before}; and it is given to them in resemblance. There for them are pure companions; there forever they abide.

26. Allāh disdains {dislikes} not to use the similitude of things, lowest as well as highest. Those who believe know that it is truth from their Lord; but those who reject Faith say: "What means Allāh by this similitude {*Mathalan*: resemblance}?" By it, He causes many to stray, and many He leads into the right path; but He causes not to stray, except those who forsake (the path) {*al-Fāsiqīn*}.

26. Lo! Allāh disdains {dislikes} not to coin the similitude {example} even of a gnat {insect}. Those who believe know that it is the truth from their Lord; but those who disbelieve say: What does Allāh wish (to teach) by such a similitude? He misleads many thereby, and He guides many thereby; and He misleads hereby only miscreants;

27. Those who break Allāh's Covenant {oath} after it is ratified {approved, accepted} and who sunder {break} what Allāh has ordered to be joined, and do mischief on earth: These cause loss (only) to themselves {*Khāsirūn*}

27. Those who break the covenant {oath, promise {of Allāh after ratifying {accepting} it and sever {break} that which Allāh ordered to be joined, and (who) make mischief in the earth: Those are they who are the losers

28. How can you reject the faith in Allāh? - Seeing that you were without life, and He gave you life; then, will He cause you to die, and will again bring you to life; and again to Him will you return.

28. How disbelieve you in Allāh when you were dead and He gave life to you! Then He will give you death, then life again, and then unto Him you will return.

29. It is He Who has created for you all things that are on earth; then He turned to heaven and made them into seven firmament {regions} And of all things he has perfect knowledge.

29. He it is Who created for you all that is in the earth. Then turned He to the heaven, and fashioned it as seven heavens. And He is Knower of all things.

EXPLANATION

21: For an explanation of *Taqwā*, see note 2:2. Adoration is the highest and humblest act of reverence and worship. When you develop that relationship with God, your faith produces works of righteousness, and your whole nature will be transformed.

22: Further proofs of God's goodness to you are provided in this verse. Your whole life, physical and spiritual, depends upon Him. The spiritual is represented by the "Canopy of Heaven". The truth has been brought plainly before you. Will you still resist it and go after false gods, the creations of your own fancy? One's false gods may be idols, superstitions, Self, or even great or glorious things like Poetry, Art, or Science, which can all be set up as rivals to God. They may be pride of race, pride of birth, pride of wealth or position, pride of power, pride of learning, or even spiritual pride.

23: Here is a concrete test of Qur'anic revelation. Can you produce one *Sūrah* like it? If there is anyone besides God who can inspire spiritual truth in such noble language, produce your evidence.

24: If by one's own efforts, he cannot match the spiritual light, and yet, obstinately rejects true faith, then there will be a fire in his soul, the punishment that will burn up all his cherished idols. This fire consumes both the worshipper and that which he falsely worships. He cannot escape from it, even if he imagines himself reduced to a lifeless object like a stick or stone; for it is all-devouring.

25: If Fire is the symbol of Punishment, the Garden is the symbol of Reward. And what could be more delightful than a Garden where you observe from a scenic height a beautiful landscape around you - rivers flowing with crystal water, and fruit trees which bear the choicest fruits. You think, because of your past experience of the world, it is the same, but it is much better. Then there is the companionship of *Muṭahharatun* "pure and holy". The Companionship is that of souls and applies to both sexes in the physical world of men and women. This joy will abide beyond the realms of Time.

26-27: The word for "the lowest" in the original Arabic means "gnat", a byword in the Arabic language for the weakest of creatures. In 29:41, which was revealed before this *Sūrah*, the similitude of the spider was used, and similarly in 22:73, there is the similitude of the fly. (For similitudes taken from magnificent forces of nature, expressed in exalted language, see 2:19 above.) To God, all His creation has some special meaning appropriate to itself, and some of what we consider the lowest creatures also have wonderful qualities. Verses 26 and 27 form one sentence and should be read together. "Forsaking the path" is defined in 2:27, viz., breaking solemn covenants which the sinner's own soul had ratified before the beginning of time, see 7:172 verse and notes). This causes division among humankind. The makers of mischief on earth will be sure losers in the Hereafter.

28-29: In the preceding verses, God has used various arguments. He has recalled His goodness (2:21-22); resolved doubts (2:23); plainly set forth the penalty for wrongdoing (2:24); given glad tidings (2:25), shown how misunderstandings arise from a deliberate rejection of the light and breach of the Covenant (2: 26-27). Now (2:28-29), He pleads with His creatures and appeals to their own subjective feelings. He brought you into being. When you die on this earth, you will return to Him. The immeasurable depths of space above and around you may be staggering, yet they are part of His plan. What you have imagined as the seven firmament (and any other scheme you may construct) bears witness to His design of order and perfection. His knowledge (unlike yours) is all-comprehending.

IMPORTANT POINTS TO LEARN AND REFLECT UPON

- We must worship Allāh ﷻ and have *Taqwā.*

- The Qur'ān is a miracle, and no one can produce a book like this.

- All the creation of Allāh ﷻ testify to His Greatness.

ARABIC GLOSSARY WORDS

بِسْمِ اللهِ الرَّحْمٰنِ الرَّحِيمِ

يٰاَيُّهَا النَّاسُ (21)	O people	تَعْلَمُونَ	know
اعْبُدُوا	worship	(23) وَ إِنْ	And if
رَبَّكُمُ	your Lord	كُنْتُمْ	you are
الَّذِى	Who	فِى رَيْبٍ	in doubt
خَلَقَكُمْ	created you	مِمَّا	concerning what
وَ الَّذِينَ	and those who were	نَزَّلْنَا	We sent down
مِنْ قَبْلِكُمْ	before you	عَلٰى عَبْدِنَا	on Our servant
لَعَلَّكُمْ	maybe you	فَأْتُوا	so bring
تَتَّقُونَ	become *muttaqi*	بِسُورَةٍ	a *surah*
الَّذِى جَعَلَ (22)	Who made	مِن مِّثْلِهِ	like it
لَكُمُ	for you	وَ ادْعُوا	and call
الْأَرْضَ	the earth	شُهَدَآءَكُمْ	your witnesses
فِرَاشًا	a bed	مِنْ دُونِ اللهِ	other than Allah
وَّ السَّمَآءَ	and the heaven	إِنْ كُنْتُمْ	if you are
بِنَآءً	a building	صٰدِقِينَ	truthful
وَّ أَنْزَلَ	and sent down	(24) فَإِنْ	So if
مِنَ السَّمَآءِ	from the sky	لَمْ تَفْعَلُوا	you did (could) not do
مَآءً	water	وَ لَنْ تَفْعَلُوا	and you will never (be able to) do
فَأَخْرَجَ بِهِ	so He brought out with it (water)	فَاتَّقُوا	then fear
مِنَ الثَّمَرٰتِ	(from) the fruits	النَّارَ	the fire (Hell)
رِزْقًا	as sustenance	الَّتِي	whose
لَكُمْ	for you	وَ قُودُهَا	fuel is
فَلَا تَجْعَلُوا	so do not make	النَّاسُ	the people
لله	for Allah	وَ الْحِجَارَةُ	and the stones
أَنْدَادًا	equals	أُعِدَّتْ	it is prepared
وَّ أَنْتُمْ	while you	لِلْكٰفِرِينَ	for the disbelievers

(25) وَ بَشِّرِ	And give good news	أَنْ يَّضْرِبَ	that He uses
الَّذِينَ اٰمَنُوْا	(to) those who believed	مَثَلًا مَّا	an example like
وَعَمِلُوا	and did	بَعُوْضَةً	a mosquito
الصّٰلِحٰتِ	righteous deeds	فَمَا فَوْقَهَا	and even more (insignificant) than it
أَنَّ لَهُمْ	indeed for them there are	فَأَمَّا الَّذِينَ	so as for those (are concerned) who
جَنّٰتٍ	gardens	اٰمَنُوْا	believed
تَجْرِى	run	فَيَعْلَمُوْنَ	they shall (come to) know
مِنْ تَحْتِهَا	underneath these (gardens)	أَنَّهُ الْحَقُّ	that it is the truth
الْأَنْهٰرُ	the rivers	مِنْ رَّبِّهِمْ	from their Lord
كُلَّمَا	whenever	وَ أَمَّا الَّذِينَ	whereas those who
رُزِقُوْا	they are provided	كَفَرُوا	disbelieved
مِنْهَا	therefrom	فَيَقُوْلُوْنَ	so they shall say
مِنْ ثَمَرَةٍ	with fruits	مَاذَآ	what
رِزْقًا	as provision	أَرَادَ اللَّهُ	does Allah mean
قَالُوا	they say	بِهٰذَا مَثَلًا	with this example
هٰذَا الَّذِى	this is what	يُضِلُّ بِهِ	He misleads with it
رُزِقْنَا	we were provided	كَثِيْرًا	many
مِنْ قَبْلُ	earlier	وَّ يَهْدِى بِهِ	and He guides with it
وَ أُتُوا	and they are granted	كَثِيْرًا	many
بِهِ مُتَشَابِهًا	similar to it	وَمَا يُضِلُّ بِهِ	and He causes not to stray with it
وَ لَهُمْ	and for them	إِلَّا الْفٰسِقِيْنَ	except the vicious
فِيْهَآ	in it (in Paradise)	(27) الَّذِينَ يَنْقُضُوْنَ	Those who break
أَزْوَاجٌ	spouses	عَهْدَ اللهِ	the covenant of Allah
مُطَهَّرَةٌ	purified	مِنْ بَعْدِ	after
وَّ هُمْ	and they	مِيْثَاقِهِ	binding it
فِيْهَا خٰلِدُوْنَ	shall ever remain in it	وَ يَقْطَعُوْنَ	and they cut asunder
(26) إِنَّ اللهَ	Indeed Allah	مَآ أَمَرَ اللهُ بِهِ	what Allah ordered
لَا يَسْتَحْىٖ	is not ashamed	أَنْ يُّوْصَلَ	that it be joined

وَيُفْسِدُونَ	and they create corruption	خَلَقَ	Who created
فِى ٱلْأَرْضِ	in the earth	لَكُم مَّا	for you what is
أُوْلَـٰئِكَ هُمُ	those, they are	فِي ٱلْأَرْضِ	in the earth
ٱلْخَـٰسِرُونَ	the losers	جَمِيعًا	all (of you)
(28) كَيْفَ	How	ثُمَّ ٱسْتَوَىٰ	then He turned (lit. straightened)
تَكْفُرُونَ بِٱللَّهِ	(do) you disbelieve in Allah	إِلَى ٱلسَّمَآءِ	to the Heaven
وَكُنتُمْ أَمْوَٰتًا	and you were dead	فَسَوَّىٰهُنَّ	so He fashioned
فَأَحْيَاكُمْ	and He gave life to you	سَبْعَ سَمَـٰوَٰتٍ	seven heavens
ثُمَّ يُمِيتُكُمْ	then He will put you to death	وَ هُوَ	and He is
ثُمَّ يُحْيِيكُمْ	and again He shall give you life	بِكُلِّ شَيْءٍ	with everything
ثُمَّ إِلَيْهِ تُرْجَعُونَ	then to Him you shall be returned	عَلِيمٌ	All-knowing
(29) هُوَ ٱلَّذِى	He is the One		

SECTION -4-

Surah Al-Baqarah
2: 30-39

THE TEXT OF THE QUR'ĀN

بِسۡمِ ٱللَّهِ ٱلرَّحۡمَٰنِ ٱلرَّحِيمِ

وَإِذۡ قَالَ رَبُّكَ لِلۡمَلَٰٓئِكَةِ إِنِّي جَاعِلٌ فِي ٱلۡأَرۡضِ خَلِيفَةً

قَالُوٓاْ أَتَجۡعَلُ فِيهَا مَن يُفۡسِدُ فِيهَا وَيَسۡفِكُ ٱلدِّمَآءَ وَنَحۡنُ

نُسَبِّحُ بِحَمۡدِكَ وَنُقَدِّسُ لَكَ قَالَ إِنِّي أَعۡلَمُ مَا لَا تَعۡلَمُونَ

﴿٣٠﴾ وَعَلَّمَ ءَادَمَ ٱلۡأَسۡمَآءَ كُلَّهَا ثُمَّ عَرَضَهُمۡ عَلَى ٱلۡمَلَٰٓئِكَةِ

فَقَالَ أَنۢبِئُونِي بِأَسۡمَآءِ هَٰٓؤُلَآءِ إِن كُنتُمۡ صَٰدِقِينَ ﴿٣١﴾ قَالُوٓاْ

سُبۡحَٰنَكَ لَا عِلۡمَ لَنَآ إِلَّا مَا عَلَّمۡتَنَآ إِنَّكَ أَنتَ ٱلۡعَلِيمُ ٱلۡحَكِيمُ

﴿٣٢﴾ قَالَ يَٰٓـَٔادَمُ أَنۢبِئۡهُم بِأَسۡمَآئِهِمۡ فَلَمَّآ أَنۢبَأَهُم بِأَسۡمَآئِهِمۡ قَالَ

أَلَمۡ أَقُل لَّكُمۡ إِنِّيٓ أَعۡلَمُ غَيۡبَ ٱلسَّمَٰوَٰتِ وَٱلۡأَرۡضِ وَأَعۡلَمُ مَا

تُبۡدُونَ وَمَا كُنتُمۡ تَكۡتُمُونَ ﴿٣٣﴾ وَإِذۡ قُلۡنَا لِلۡمَلَٰٓئِكَةِ ٱسۡجُدُواْ

لِأٓدَمَ فَسَجَدُوٓاْ إِلَّآ إِبۡلِيسَ أَبَىٰ وَٱسۡتَكۡبَرَ وَكَانَ مِنَ ٱلۡكَٰفِرِينَ

﴿٣٤﴾ وَقُلۡنَا يَٰٓـَٔادَمُ ٱسۡكُنۡ أَنتَ وَزَوۡجُكَ ٱلۡجَنَّةَ وَكُلَا مِنۡهَا رَغَدًا

حَيۡثُ شِئۡتُمَا وَلَا تَقۡرَبَا هَٰذِهِ ٱلشَّجَرَةَ فَتَكُونَا مِنَ ٱلظَّٰلِمِينَ ﴿٣٥﴾

فَأَزَلَّهُمَا ٱلشَّيۡطَٰنُ عَنۡهَا فَأَخۡرَجَهُمَا مِمَّا كَانَا فِيهِ وَقُلۡنَا ٱهۡبِطُواْ

بَعْضُكُمْ لِبَعْضٍ عَدُوٌّ وَلَكُمْ فِي الْأَرْضِ مُسْتَقَرٌّ وَمَتَاعٌ إِلَى حِينٍ ﴿٣٦﴾ فَتَلَقَّى آدَمُ مِن رَّبِّهِ كَلِمَاتٍ فَتَابَ عَلَيْهِ إِنَّهُ هُوَ التَّوَّابُ الرَّحِيمُ ﴿٣٧﴾ قُلْنَا اهْبِطُوا مِنْهَا جَمِيعًا فَإِمَّا يَأْتِيَنَّكُم مِّنِّي هُدًى فَمَن تَبِعَ هُدَايَ فَلَا خَوْفٌ عَلَيْهِمْ وَلَا هُمْ يَحْزَنُونَ ﴿٣٨﴾ وَالَّذِينَ كَفَرُوا وَكَذَّبُوا بِآيَاتِنَا أُولَٰئِكَ أَصْحَابُ النَّارِ هُمْ فِيهَا خَالِدُونَ ﴿٣٩﴾

TRANSLATIONS

Section 4: 30-39 (A. Y. Ali)

30. Behold, your Lord {*Rabb*} said to the angels: "I will create a vicegerent {*Khalifah*} on earth." They said: "Will you place therein one who will make mischief therein and shed blood? - While we do celebrate Your praises and glorify Your holy (name)." He said: "I know what you know not."

31. And He taught Ādam the names {*`asmā'*} of all things; then He placed him before the angels, and said: "Tell Me the names {*`asmā'*} of these if you are right.

32. They said: "Glory to You: of knowledge, we have none, save what You have taught us: in truth, it is You who is perfect in knowledge and wisdom."

33. He said: "O Ādam! Tell them their names." When he had told them, Allāh said: "Did I not tell you that I know the secrets of heaven and earth, and I know what you reveal and what you conceal?"

34. And behold, We said to the angels: "Bow down to Ādam:" and they bowed down: not so *Iblis* {Satan}: he refused and was haughty {proud}: he was of those who

Section 4: 30-39 (M. M. Pickthall)

30. And when your Lord said unto the angels: Lo! I am about to place a viceroy in the earth, they said: Will You place therein one who will do harm therein and will shed blood, while we, hymn Your praise and sanctify {make holy} You? He said: Surely, I know that which you know not.

31. And He taught Ādam all the names, then showed them to the angels, saying: Inform me of the names {*`asmā'*} of these, if you are truthful.

32. They said: Be glorified! We have no knowledge saving that which You have taught us. Lo! You, only You, are the Knower, the Wise.

33. He said: O Ādam! Inform them of their names, and when he had informed of their names, He said: Did I not tell you that I know the secret of the heavens and the earth? And I know that which you disclose and which you hide.

34. And when We said unto the angels: Prostrate {bow down} yourselves before Ādam, they fell prostrate, all except *Iblis* {Satan}. He demurred {refused} through

reject Faith.

35. We said: "O Ādam! Dwell you and your wife in the Garden; and eat of the bountiful things therein as (where and when) you will; but approach not this tree, or you run into harm and transgression {*Az-Zulm*: offence}"

36. Then did Satan make them slip from the (Garden), and get them out of the state (of felicity) in which they had been. We said: "Get you down, all (you people), with enmity between yourselves. On earth will be your dwelling place and your means of livelihood - for a time."

37. Then learned Ādam from his Lord words of inspiration {*Kalimātin*}, and his Lord turned towards him; for He is Oft-Returning {*At-Tawwāb*}, Most-Merciful {*Ar-Rahīm*}

38. We said: "Get you down all from here: and if, as is sure, there comes to you guidance from Me, whosoever follows My guidance, on them shall be no fear, nor shall they grieve."

39. "But those who reject Faith and belie {disprove} Our Signs, they shall be Companions of the Fire; they shall abide therein."

pride, and so became a disbeliever.

35. And We said: O Ādam! Dwell you and your wife in the Garden, and eat you freely (of the fruits) thereof where you will; but come not near this tree least you become wrongdoers.

36. But Satan caused them to deflect {divert} therefrom and expelled them from the (happy) state in which they were; and We said: Fall down, one of you a foe unto the other! There shall be for you on earth a habitation and provision {means for livelihood} for a time.

37. Then Ādam received from his Lord words (of revelation), and He relented {asked forgiveness} toward him. Lo! He is the Relenting, the Merciful.

38. We said: Go down, all of you, from hence; but verily, there comes unto you from Me a guidance; and whosoever follows My guidance, there shall no fear come upon them neither shall they grieve.

39. But they who disbelieve, and deny our revelations, such are rightful owners of the Fire. They will abide therein.

EXPLANATION

30: (Verses 30-39 describe the story of creation.) It would seem that the angels, though holy and pure, are without passion or emotion, of which the highest flower is love. If humankind was to be endowed with emotions and knowledge, it would lead them to the highest and bring them down to the lowest. The power of will, the ability to choose between good and evil, permits humans a mastery over their own fortunes. It grants them control over nature, thus bringing them nearer to the Godlike nature, which has supreme mastery and will. The angels, in their one-sidedness, saw only the mischief that independence would cause and the humans' potential to misuse their emotional nature. We must not imagine the angels as being jealous; they were without full understanding of Divine purpose. At the same time, the matter is brought home to them when the actual capacities of human are shown to them (2:31,33).

31-32: The literal words in Arabic throughout this passage are: "The names of things" which commentators take to mean the inner nature and qualities of things, and things here would include feelings. Humankind was thus able to love and understand love, and thus plan and initiate, as befitting the office of *Khalīfah*, the vicegerent on earth. The angels acknowledged their limitation of knowledge. Human beings are thus given many qualities which are latent in each human and can be activated and brought to full perfection. These may also be destroyed by neglect and may lead to one's own detriment.

33: {Ādam demonstrated his knowledge by telling the name of things, thus proving his superiority to the angels in this regard. Still, no one can fully understand the purpose of God in all His creation. Both angels and humans have to acknowledge their limitations and accept His plan as revealed in nature and in His Books. AG}

34:   The Arabic may also be translated: "They bowed down, except *Iblīs*." In that case, *Iblīs* (Satan) would be one of the angels. In 18:50, *Iblīs* is spoken of as a Jinn, a creature made of fire. We shall discuss later the meaning of this word.

35:   Was the Garden of Eden a place on this earth? Obviously not, for as we see in verse 36 below, it was after the fall that the judgement was pronounced: "On earth will be your dwelling." Before the fall, we must suppose humans to have been on another plane altogether - one of innocence and a spiritual existence, without evil or want of faith. The Garden and the tree are allegorical. The forbidden tree was not the tree of knowledge for the human was given in that perfect state fuller knowledge than he has now (2:31; it was the tree of Evil. –ulm in Arabic implies harm, wrong, injustice, and may have reference to oneself; when the wrong is done to others, it implies tyranny and oppression.

36:   The *Iblīs*, the Satan in 2:34 is apparently the Power of Evil, with the root idea of rebellion against God. Also, "slipping" from the Garden represents not only their exit, but also the idea of Evil gradually tempting humans and bringing him down from a higher to a lower state. Note the transition in Arabic from the singular number in 2:33, to the dual in 2:35, and the plural here, which I have indicated in English by "All you people." Evidently, Ādam is the arch-type of all humankind, and the sexes go together in all spiritual matters.

{It must be noted that the Qur'ān, unlike the Bible, does not hold women responsible for insinuating Ādam and committing the act of disobedience. Both Ādam and Eve committed a mistake, both were punished, and both were forgiven. Besides, their mistake was not unforgivable. In Islam, there is no concept of "Original Sin", and no need for the sacrifice of Jesus, who, according to Christian faith, was the son of God. Thus, human destiny on earth is not the result of the Fall of Ādam, but the fulfillment of his mission as vicegerent on earth. AG} Human destiny on earth in this lower state is for a time. But we must fulfil our earthly duties also. Our earthly duties, too, are a part of our spiritual goal.

37:   *Kalimātin*, the "words" here mean "inspiration," and "spiritual knowledge". The Arabic word *Talaqqa*, used for "learn" here implies some effort on his part to which God's Grace responded. {The episode teaches humans their true nature of often erring but always turning to God and finding Divine Mercy ever ready to accept their repentance. In Islam, this relationship between God humans does not require a priest, intermediary or human sacrifice. AG}

38:   Note the transition from the plural "We" at the beginning of the verse to the singular "Me" later in the same verse. God speaks of Himself usually in the first person plural "We" - it is the plural of respect and honor and is used in human language in Royal proclamations and decrees. But where a special personal relationship is expressed, the singular "I" or "Me" is used, see 26:52 etc.

39:   But if the soul, in spite of the Oft-Returning Mercy of God, rejects the higher light of faith, the inevitable result must be the abiding Fire of Divine anger.

IMPORTANT POINTS TO LEARN AND REFLECT UPON

- Allāh created Ādam as His *Khalīfah* on earth and gave him knowledge.

- *Iblīs*, the Satan defied Allāh's commands and he became one of those who reject faith.

- Ādam and Hawwā made a mistake. They asked for Allāh's forgiveness, and Allāh forgave them.

ARABIC GLOSSARY WORDS

بِسْمِ اللهِ اَلرَّحْمٰنِ اَلرَّحِيمِ

وَ إِذْ (30)	And when	عَرَضَهُمْ	He presented them
قَالَ رَبُّكَ	your Lord said	عَلَى الْمَلَـٰئِكَةِ	on (to) the angels
لِلْمَلَـٰئِكَةِ	to the angels	فَقَالَ	then He said
إِنِّى جَاعِلٌ	I am going to appoint (make)	أَنْبِئُونِى	tell Me
فِى الْأَرْضِ	in (on) the Earth	بِأَسْمَاءِ	names of
خَلِيفَةً	a vicegerent	هَـٰؤُلَاءِ	these
قَالُوا	they said	إِنْ كُنْتُمْ صَٰدِقِينَ	if you are truthful
أَتَجْعَلُ	are You going to appoint	قَالُوا (32)	They said
فِيهَا	in it	سُبْحَٰنَكَ	Glory be to You
مَنْ يُفْسِدُ	one who will do corruption	لَا عِلْمَ لَنَا	no knowledge for (with) us
فِيهَا	in it	إِلَّا	except
وَ يَسْفِكُ	and (who) will shed	مَا عَلَّمْتَنَا	what You taught us
الدِّمَاءَ	the blood	إِنَّكَ أَنْتَ	indeed You are
وَ نَحْنُ	and we	الْعَلِيمُ	the All-Knowing
نُسَبِّحُ	glorify You	الْحَكِيمُ	the All-Wise
بِحَمْدِكَ	with Your praise	قَالَ (33)	He said
وَ نُقَدِّسُ	and we sanctify	يَٰٓأَٰدَمُ	O Adam
لَكَ	to You	أَنْبِئْهُمْ	tell them
قَالَ	He said	بِأَسْمَآئِهِمْ	names of these
إِنِّى أَعْلَمُ	I know	فَلَمَّا	so when
مَا لَا تَعْلَمُونَ	what you do not know	أَنْبَاهُمْ	he informed them
وَعَلَّمَ (31)	And He taught	بِأَسْمَائِهِمْ	with their names
أَٰدَمَ	Adam	قَالَ	He said
الْأَسْمَاءَ	the names	أَلَمْ أَقُلْ لَكُمْ	did I not tell you?
كُلَّهَا	all of them	إِنِّى أَعْلَمُ	I know
ثُمَّ	then	غَيْبَ	the hidden (reality)

اَلسَّمٰوٰتِ	(of) the heavens	اَلشَّيْطٰنُ	the Satan
وَ الْأَرْضِ	and the Earth	عَنْهَا	from it (this saying)
وَ أَعْلَمُ	and I know	فَأَخْرَجَهُمَا	thus he made (both of) them come ou
مَا تُبْدُونَ	what you disclose	مِمَّا	from (the state in) which
وَمَا كُنْتُمْ تَكْتُمُونَ	and what you were concealing	كَانَا	they (both) were
وَ إِذْ قُلْنَا لِلْمَلٰئِكَةِ (34)	And when We said to angels	فِيهِ	in it
اسْجُدُوا	prostrate	وَ قُلْنَا	and We said
لِأٰدَمَ	to Adam	اهْبِطُوا	get down
فَسَجَدُوا	so they prostrated	بَعْضُكُمْ لِبَعْضٍ	you are to each other
إِلَّا إِبْلِيسَ	except Iblis		(lit. some of you to some)
أَبٰى	he refused	عَدُوٌّ	enemy
وَ اسْتَكْبَرَ	and acted arrogantly	وَ لَكُمْ فِى الْأَرْضِ	and for you in the Earth
وَكَانَ	and he was (became)	مُسْتَقَرٌّ	is a place to stay
مِنَ الْكٰفِرِينَ	from (the disbelieved)	وَمَتَاعٌ	and a provision
وَ قُلْنَا (35)	And We said	إِلٰى حِينٍ	for a time
يٰأٰدَمُ	O Adam	فَتَلَقّٰى أٰدَمُ (37)	Then Adam learned
اسْكُنْ	inhabit	مِنْ رَّبِّهِ	from his Lord
أَنْتَ وَزَوْجُكَ	you and your spouse	كَلِمٰتٍ	words
الْجَنَّةَ	the Garden	فَتَابَ	so He turned (accepted *tawbah*)
وَكُلَا	and you both eat	عَلَيْهِ	toward him
مِنْهَا	from it	إِنَّهُ, هُوَ	indeed He is
رَغَدًا	freely/abundantly (happily)	التَّوَّابُ	the Oft-Returning
حَيْثُ	wherever	الرَّحِيمُ	the Most Merciful
شِئْتُمَا	you (both) want	قُلْنَا (38)	We said
وَ لَا تَقْرَبَا	and you (both) should not go near	اهْبِطُوا	get down
هٰذِهِ الشَّجَرَةَ	this tree	مِنْهَا	from it
فَتَكُونَا	so you (both) may become	جَمِيعًا	all (of you)
مِنَ الظّٰلِمِينَ	from the unjust people	فَإِمَّا	so whenever
فَأَزَلَّهُمَا (36)	Then caused to slip (both of) them	يَأْتِيَنَّكُمْ	comes to you (as is sure)

مِنِّى	from Me	يَحْزَنُونَ	worry
هُدًى	Guidance	وَ الَّذِينَ كَفَرُوا	(39) And those who disbelieved
فَمَنْ	so whoever	وَكَذَّبُوا	and rejected (said that it is a lie)
تَبِعَ	follows	بِآيَاتِنَا	Our signs
هُدَايَ	My guidance	أُولَٰئِكَ	those are
فَلَا خَوْفٌ	so no fear	أَصْحَابُ النَّارِ	the companions of the fire
عَلَيْهِمْ	on them	هُمْ فِيهَا	they shall be in it
وَ لَا هُمْ	(and) nor shall they	خَالِدُونَ	shall ever remain

SECTION -5-

Sūrah Al-Baqarah
2: 40-46

THE TEXT OF THE QUR'ĀN

بِسْمِ اللَّهِ الرَّحْمَٰنِ الرَّحِيمِ

يَٰبَنِىٓ إِسْرَٰٓءِيلَ ٱذْكُرُوا۟ نِعْمَتِىَ ٱلَّتِىٓ أَنْعَمْتُ عَلَيْكُمْ وَأَوْفُوا۟ بِعَهْدِىٓ أُوفِ بِعَهْدِكُمْ وَإِيَّٰىَ فَٱرْهَبُونِ ۝ وَءَامِنُوا۟ بِمَآ أَنزَلْتُ مُصَدِّقًا لِّمَا مَعَكُمْ وَلَا تَكُونُوٓا۟ أَوَّلَ كَافِرٍۭ بِهِۦ ۖ وَلَا تَشْتَرُوا۟ بِـَٔايَٰتِى ثَمَنًا قَلِيلًا وَإِيَّٰىَ فَٱتَّقُونِ ۝ وَلَا تَلْبِسُوا۟ ٱلْحَقَّ بِٱلْبَٰطِلِ وَتَكْتُمُوا۟ ٱلْحَقَّ وَأَنتُمْ تَعْلَمُونَ ۝ وَأَقِيمُوا۟ ٱلصَّلَوٰةَ وَءَاتُوا۟ ٱلزَّكَوٰةَ وَٱرْكَعُوا۟ مَعَ ٱلرَّٰكِعِينَ ۝ أَتَأْمُرُونَ ٱلنَّاسَ بِٱلْبِرِّ وَتَنسَوْنَ أَنفُسَكُمْ وَأَنتُمْ تَتْلُونَ ٱلْكِتَٰبَ ۚ أَفَلَا تَعْقِلُونَ ۝ وَٱسْتَعِينُوا۟ بِٱلصَّبْرِ وَٱلصَّلَوٰةِ ۚ وَإِنَّهَا لَكَبِيرَةٌ إِلَّا عَلَى ٱلْخَٰشِعِينَ ۝ ٱلَّذِينَ يَظُنُّونَ أَنَّهُم مُّلَٰقُوا۟ رَبِّهِمْ وَأَنَّهُمْ إِلَيْهِ رَٰجِعُونَ ۝

TRANSLATIONS

Section 5: 40-46 (A. Y. Ali)

40.　　O Children of Israel! Call to mind the (special) favor which I bestowed upon you, and fulfil your Covenant with Me as I fulfil My Covenant with you, and fear none but Me.

41.　　And believe in what I reveal, confirming the revelation which is with you, and

Section 5: 40-46 (M. M. Pickthall)

40.　　O Children of Israel! Remember My favor wherewith I favored you, and fulfil your (part of the) covenant, I shall fulfil My (part of the) covenant, and fear Me.

41.　　And believe in that which I reveal, confirming that which you possess already (of

be not the first to reject Faith therein, nor sell My Signs for a small price; and fear Me, and Me alone.

42. And cover not Truth with falsehood, nor conceal the Truth when you know (what it is).

43. And be steadfast in prayers {*Salāh*}; practice regular charity {*Zakāh*}; and bow down your heads {*Rukū*} with those who bow down (in worship).

44. Do you enjoin right conduct on the people, and forget (to practice it) yourselves. And yet you study the Scripture? Will you not understand?

45. Truly, seek (Allāh's) help with patient perseverance {persistence} and prayer: it is indeed hard, except to those who bring a lowly spirit -

46. Who bear in mind the certainty that they are to meet their Lord, and that they are to return to Him.

the Scripture), and be not first to disbelieve therein, and part not with My revelations for a trifling {small} price, and keep your duty unto Me.

42. Confound not truth with falsehood, nor knowingly conceal the truth.

43. Establish worship, pay the poor-due, and bow your heads with those who bow (in worship).

44. Do you enjoin righteousness upon mankind while you yourselves forget (to practice it)? And you are readers of the Scripture! Have you then no sense?

45. Seek help in patience and prayer; and truly it is hard save for the humble-minded,

46. Who know that they will have to meet their Lord, and that unto Him they are returning.

EXPLANATION

40: The appeal is made to Israel in terms of their own history. You have forgotten My favors and Covenant with Me: I have fulfilled My part of the Covenant; how have you fulfilled your part of the Covenant? If you fear Me, nothing else will matter.

41: You received revelations before: now comes the Qur'ān, the final revelation, confirming them. Its first appeal should be to you: are you to be the first to reject it? And reject it for small worldly gains and national pride.

42: {The Jews had been waiting for a prophet to come and most of them recognized the truth of the final revelation and the final messenger, but their national pride prevented them from accepting it. AG}.

43: Although the argument is addressed to the Jews, it may be applied universally, as are all the teachings of the Qur'ān.

44: {It criticizes the Israelites for asking others to be righteous and themselves not acting accordingly. The Qur'ān enjoins upon Muslims to have the same consistency in their beliefs and actions also. See *Aṣ-Ṣaff* 61:2-3 .AG}

45: The Arabic word *Ṣabr* implies (1) patience; (2) constancy and steadfastness; (3) a cheerful attitude of accepting suffering with firmness of faith.

46: {Patience and prayer is hard for unbelievers, but for the believers who are sure of meeting their Lord on the Day of Judgment, it is easy. "The Prayer," Prophet Muḥammad ﷺ said "is the ascension of a believer .AG}

IMPORTANT POINTS TO LEARN AND REFLECT UPON

- Allāh ﷻ reminds the Banū Isrā'il of His many favors bestowed upon them, and asks them to fulfill their Covenant with Him.

- Those who enjoin right conduct upon other people should not forget to practice it themselves.

- In the affairs of our life, we must seek help from Allāh ﷻ through the *Ṣabr* (Patience) and the *Ṣalah* (the prayer).

ARABIC GLOSSARY WORDS

بِسْمِ اللهِ الرَّحْمٰنِ الرَّحِيمِ

يٰبَنِيَ إِسْرَآءِيلَ	(40) O Children of Israel	وَ إِيَّايَ	and Me alone
اُذْكُرُوا	remember	فَاتَّقُونِ	(so) fear (Me) (have My *taqwa*)
نِعْمَتِيَ	My Favor	وَ لَا تَلْبِسُوا	(42) And do not cover
الَّتِيَ اَنْعَمْتُ	I blessed	الْحَقَّ	the truth
عَلَيْكُمْ	you with	بِالْبَاطِلِ	with falsehood
وَ اَوْفُوا	and fulfil	وَ تَكْتُمُوا الْحَقَّ	nor hide the truth
بِعَهْدِيَ	My covenant	وَ اَنْتُمْ تَعْلَمُونَ	and you know
اُوفِ	I shall fulfil	وَ اَقِيمُوا	(43) And establish
بِعَهْدِكُمْ	your covenent	الصَّلٰوةَ	the prayer
وَ إِيَّايَ فَارْهَبُونِ	and Me alone you fear	وَ اٰتُوا	and give
وَ اٰمِنُوا	(41) And believe	الزَّكٰوةَ	Az-zakah, the poor-due
بِمَا اَنْزَلْتُ	in what I sent down	وَ ارْكَعُوا	and bow down
مُصَدِّقًا	testifying	مَعَ الرّٰكِعِينَ	with those who bow down
لِمَا مَعَكُمْ	(to) what you have (lit. what is with you)	اَتَأْمُرُونَ	(44) Do you enjoin
		النَّاسَ	the people
وَ لَا تَكُونُوا	and do not become	بِالْبِرِّ	to be virtuous (lit. with virtue)
اَوَّلَ	first	وَ تَنْسَوْنَ	and you forget
كَافِرٍ بِهِ	to disbelieve it	اَنْفُسَكُمْ	yourselves
وَ لَا تَشْتَرُوا	and do not buy (sell)	وَ اَنْتُمْ	and you
بِاٰيٰتِي	with My Signs	تَتْلُونَ	recite
ثَمَنًا قَلِيلًا	(at) a low price	الْكِتٰبَ	the Book

(46) اَلَّذِينَ	Those who
يَظُنُّونَ	think, believe
أَنَّهُمْ	that (indeed) they are
مُلَٰقُوا	going to meet
رَبِّهِمْ	their Lord
وَ أَنَّهُمْ	and that (indeed) they
إِلَيْهِ رَٰجِعُونَ	shall return to Him
أَفَلاَ تَعْقِلُونَ	so do you not understand?
(45) وَ اسْتَعِينُوا	And seek help
بِالصَّبْرِ	with patience
وَ الصَّلَٰوةِ	and the prayer
وَ إِنَّهَا	and indeed it
لَكَبِيرَةٌ	is hard (lit. big)
إِلاَّ عَلَى	except on
الْخَٰشِعِينَ	(those who are) humble

SECTION -6-

Sūrah Al-Baqarah
2: 47-59

THE TEXT OF THE QUR'ĀN

بِسۡمِ اللّٰهِ الرَّحۡمٰنِ الرَّحِیۡمِ

یٰبَنِیۡۤ اِسۡرَآءِیۡلَ اذۡکُرُوۡا نِعۡمَتِیَ الَّتِیۡۤ اَنۡعَمۡتُ عَلَیۡکُمۡ وَاَنِّیۡ فَضَّلۡتُکُمۡ عَلَی الۡعٰلَمِیۡنَ ۝ وَاتَّقُوۡا یَوۡمًا لَّا تَجۡزِیۡ نَفۡسٌ عَنۡ نَّفۡسٍ شَیۡئًا وَّلَا یُقۡبَلُ مِنۡهَا شَفَاعَةٌ وَّلَا یُؤۡخَذُ مِنۡهَا عَدۡلٌ وَّلَا هُمۡ یُنۡصَرُوۡنَ ۝ وَاِذۡ نَجَّیۡنٰکُمۡ مِّنۡ اٰلِ فِرۡعَوۡنَ یَسُوۡمُوۡنَکُمۡ سُوۡٓءَ الۡعَذَابِ یُذَبِّحُوۡنَ اَبۡنَآءَکُمۡ وَیَسۡتَحۡیُوۡنَ نِسَآءَکُمۡ وَفِیۡ ذٰلِکُمۡ بَلَآءٌ مِّنۡ رَّبِّکُمۡ عَظِیۡمٌ ۝ وَاِذۡ فَرَقۡنَا بِکُمُ الۡبَحۡرَ فَاَنۡجَیۡنٰکُمۡ وَاَغۡرَقۡنَاۤ اٰلَ فِرۡعَوۡنَ وَاَنۡتُمۡ تَنۡظُرُوۡنَ ۝ وَاِذۡ وٰعَدۡنَا مُوۡسٰۤی اَرۡبَعِیۡنَ لَیۡلَةً ثُمَّ اتَّخَذۡتُمُ الۡعِجۡلَ مِنۡۢ بَعۡدِهٖ وَاَنۡتُمۡ ظٰلِمُوۡنَ ۝ ثُمَّ عَفَوۡنَا عَنۡکُمۡ مِّنۡۢ بَعۡدِ ذٰلِکَ لَعَلَّکُمۡ تَشۡکُرُوۡنَ ۝ وَاِذۡ اٰتَیۡنَا مُوۡسَی الۡکِتٰبَ وَالۡفُرۡقَانَ لَعَلَّکُمۡ تَهۡتَدُوۡنَ ۝ وَاِذۡ قَالَ مُوۡسٰی لِقَوۡمِهٖ یٰقَوۡمِ اِنَّکُمۡ ظَلَمۡتُمۡ اَنۡفُسَکُمۡ بِاتِّخَاذِکُمُ الۡعِجۡلَ فَتُوۡبُوۡۤا اِلٰی بَارِئِکُمۡ فَاقۡتُلُوۡۤا اَنۡفُسَکُمۡ ذٰلِکُمۡ خَیۡرٌ لَّکُمۡ عِنۡدَ بَارِئِکُمۡ فَتَابَ عَلَیۡکُمۡ اِنَّهٗ هُوَ التَّوَّابُ الرَّحِیۡمُ

وَإِذْ قُلْتُمْ يَا مُوسَى لَن نُّؤْمِنَ لَكَ حَتَّى نَرَى ٱللَّهَ جَهْرَةً ﴿٥٤﴾ فَأَخَذَتْكُمُ ٱلصَّاعِقَةُ وَأَنتُمْ تَنظُرُونَ ﴿٥٥﴾ ثُمَّ بَعَثْنَاكُم مِّنۢ بَعْدِ مَوْتِكُمْ لَعَلَّكُمْ تَشْكُرُونَ ﴿٥٦﴾ وَظَلَّلْنَا عَلَيْكُمُ ٱلْغَمَامَ وَأَنزَلْنَا عَلَيْكُمُ ٱلْمَنَّ وَٱلسَّلْوَى كُلُوا۟ مِن طَيِّبَاتِ مَا رَزَقْنَاكُمْ وَمَا ظَلَمُونَا وَلَٰكِن كَانُوٓا۟ أَنفُسَهُمْ يَظْلِمُونَ ﴿٥٧﴾ وَإِذْ قُلْنَا ٱدْخُلُوا۟ هَٰذِهِ ٱلْقَرْيَةَ فَكُلُوا۟ مِنْهَا حَيْثُ شِئْتُمْ رَغَدًا وَٱدْخُلُوا۟ ٱلْبَابَ سُجَّدًا وَقُولُوا۟ حِطَّةٌ نَّغْفِرْ لَكُمْ خَطَايَاكُمْ وَسَنَزِيدُ ٱلْمُحْسِنِينَ ﴿٥٨﴾ فَبَدَّلَ ٱلَّذِينَ ظَلَمُوا۟ قَوْلًا غَيْرَ ٱلَّذِى قِيلَ لَهُمْ فَأَنزَلْنَا عَلَى ٱلَّذِينَ ظَلَمُوا۟ رِجْزًا مِّنَ ٱلسَّمَآءِ بِمَا كَانُوا۟ يَفْسُقُونَ ﴿٥٩﴾

TRANSLATIONS

Section 6: 47-59 (A. Y. Ali)

47.   O Children of Israel! Call to mind the (special) favor which I bestowed upon you, and that I preferred you to all others (for My message).

48.   Then guard yourselves {have *Taqwā*} against a day when one soul shall not avail {benefit from} another nor shall intercession {*Shafa'ah:* plea} be accepted for her, nor shall compensation be taken from her, nor shall anyone be helped (from outside).

49.   And remember, We delivered you from the people of Pharaoh: they set you hard tasks and punishments, slaughtered your sons and let your womenfolk live; therein was a

Section 6: 47-59 (M. M. Pickthall)

47.   O Children of Israel! Remember My favor wherewith I favored you, and how I preferred you to (all) creatures.

48.   And guard yourselves against a day when no soul will in aught avail {benefit from} another, nor will intercession {plea} be accepted from it, nor will compensation be received from it, nor will they be helped.

49.   And (remember) when We did deliver you from Pharaoh's folk, who were and sparing {leaving} your women: That was a tremendous trial from your Lord.

tremendous trial from your Lord.

50. And remember, We divided the Sea for you and saved you and drowned Pharaoh's people within your very sight.

51. And remember, We appointed forty nights for Moses {Musa} and in his absence, you took the calf (for worship), and you did grievous wrong.

52. Even then, We did forgive you, there was a chance for you to be grateful.

53. And remember, We gave Moses the Scripture {Al-Kitab} and the Criterion (between right and wrong) {Al-Furqan}, there was a chance for you to be guided aright.

54. And remember Moses said to his people: "O my people! You have indeed wronged yourselves by your worship of the calf: so turn (in repentance) to your Maker {Bari'} and slay yourselves (the wrongdoers); that will be better for you in the sight of your Maker." Then He turned towards you (in forgiveness): for He is Oft-Returning {At-Tawwab} Most-Merciful {Ar-Rahim}

55. And remember you said: "O Moses! We shall never believe in you until we see Allah manifestly," but you were dazed by thunder and lightning even as you looked on.

56. Then We raised you up after your death; you had the chance to be grateful.

57. And We gave You the shade of clouds and sent down to you manna and quails, saying: "Eat of the good things We have provided for you": (but they rebelled); to Us, they did no harm, but they harmed their own souls.

58. And remember, We said: "Enter this town, and eat of the plenty therein as you wish; but enter the gate with humility, in posture and in words {saying Hittatun}, and We shall forgive you your faults and increase (the portion of) those who do good."

59. But the transgressors {disobedient ones} changed the word from that which had been given them; so We sent on the trans-

50. And when We brought you through the sea and rescued you, and drowned the folk of Pharaoh in your sight.

51. And when We did appoint for Moses forty nights (of solitude), and then you chose the calf, when he had gone from you, and were wrongdoers.

52. Then, even after that, We pardoned you, in order that you might give thanks.

53. And when We gave unto Moses the Scripture and the Criterion (of right and wrong), that you might be led aright.

54. And when Moses said unto his people: O my people! You have wronged yourselves by your choosing of the calf (for worship) so turn in penitence {regret} to your Creator, and kill (the guilty) yourselves. That will be best for you with your Creator and He will relent {soften} toward you. Lo! He is the Relenting, the Merciful.

55. And when you said: O Moses! We will not believe in you till we see Allah plainly {directly}; and even while you gazed the lightning seized you.

56. Then We revived {raised} you after your extinction {death}, that you might give thanks.

57. And We caused the white cloud to overshadow you and sent down on you the manna and the quails, (saying): Eat of the good things wherewith We have provided you - We wronged them not, but they did wrong themselves.

58. And when We said: Go into this township and eat freely of that which is therein, and enter the gate prostrate {modestly}, and say: "Repentance {state of being regret for what has been done in past}." We will forgive you your sins and increase (reward) for the right-doers.

59. But those who did wrong changed the word which had been told them for another saying, and We sent down upon the

gressors a plague from heaven, for that they infringed (our command) repeatedly.

evildoers wrath from Heaven for their evil doing.

EXPLANATION

47: These words in 2:40 introduced a general account of God's favors to Israel. Now, we are introduced to accounts of some particular incidents in Israel's history.

48: The conclusion here is clear: do not think that special favors exempt you from personal responsibility.

49: The bondage in Egypt placed a burden of hard work upon Israelites. Pharaoh decreed: "Every son that is born you shall cast into the river, and every daughter you shall save alive," (Exod. 1:22). It was because of this decree that Moses was hidden three months after he was born, he was put into an ark of bulrushes and cast into the Nile, where he was found by Pharaoh's daughter and wife (28:9), and adopted into the family (Exod. 2:2-10). (See also 20:37-40.) Thus, Moses was brought up by the enemies of his people. He was chosen by God to deliver his people.

50: When the Israelites finally escaped from Egypt, they were pursued by Pharaoh and his host. By a miracle, the Israelites crossed the Red Sea, but the host of Pharaoh was drowned (Exod. 14:5-31).

51: This incident took place after the revelation to Moses of the Ten Commandments and the Laws on Mount Sinai: Moses was summoned up onto the Mount, and he was there for forty days and forty nights (Exod. 24:18). But the people got impatient and made a golden calf to worship it (Exod. 32:1-8).

52: Moses prayed for his people, and God forgave them. This is the language of the Qur'ān. The Old Testament version is more blunt (see Exod. 32:14).

53: God's revelation is the only true standard of right and wrong. In this passage, some commentators take the Scripture and the Criterion (*Al-Furqān*) to be identical. Others take them to be two distinct things: The first being the Scripture, and the other the Criterion. I agree with the latter view, (see also *Al-Anbiyā* 21:48 and *Al-Furqān* 25:1). 54: The speech of Moses may have a literal meaning, as reported in Exod. 32:27-28; resulting in the killing of 3,000 people that day. A more spiritual interpretation would be to take the meaning of "*anfusa-kum*" as "your souls" and not as "yourselves", meaning to repent earnestly.

55: As to seeing God, we have in Exod. 33:20, "And He said, you can not see My face: for no man can see Me and live." The punishment for insisting on seeing God was, therefore, death.

56: {The rejectors of faith were given a second lease on life. They were either raised from death or were given a second spiritual life after their spiritual death due to disobedience}.

57: *Manna*=Hebrew, *Manhu*: Arabic *Mahuwa*? - What is it? In Exod. 16:14, it is described as "a small round thing, as small as the frost on the ground." This is the Hebrew account, probably distorted by traditional exaggeration. The actual *Manna* found to this day in the Sinai region is a gummy, saccharine secretion found on a species of Tamarisk. As to quails, large flights of them are driven by winds in the eastern Mediterranean in certain seasons of the year.

58: This probably refers to *Shittim*. It was the "town of acacias," just east of the Jordan, where the Israelites were guilty of excesses and the worship of false gods (Num. 25:1-2, also 8-9); a terrible punishment ensued. A more general lesson to be drawn is this: in an hour of triumph, we must be humble and forgiving. Otherwise, our arrogance will draw its own punishment.

59: The word taught was *Ḥiṭṭatun*, meaning "humility and forgiveness. It was twisted to take on the opposite meaning, justifying arrogant and oppressive behavior AG}.

IMPORTANT POINTS TO LEARN AND REFLECT UPON

- Through the stories of Banī Isrā'īl, Allāh ﷻ want, to teach the Muslim 'Ummah some important lessons.

- Allāh ﷻ showed many favors to Banī Isrā'īl, yet they were consistently disobedient and thereby were punished.

- We must follow the commands of Allāh ﷻ both in words and spirit.

ARABIC GLOSSARY WORDS

بِسْمِ اللهِ الرَّحْمٰنِ الرَّحِيمِ

يَبَنِىَ إِسْرَاءِيلَ	(47) O Children of Israel		يَسُومُونَكُمْ	they affliced you
اذكُرُوا	remember		سُوَءَ الْعَذَابِ	(with) dreadful chastisement
نِعْمَتِىَ الَّتِىَ	My blessing (with) which		يُذَبِّحُونَ	they were slaughtering
أَنْعَمْتُ عَلَيْكُمْ	I blessed you		أَبْنَاءَكُمْ	your sons
وَ أَنِّى	and indeed I		وَ يَسْتَحْيُونَ	and sparing
فَضَّلْتُكُمْ	favored you		نِسَاءَكُمْ	your women
عَلَى الْعٰلَمِينَ	above all the worlds		وَفِى ذٰلِكُمْ	and in this was
وَ اتَّقُوا	(48) And fear		بَلَاءٌ	a trial
يَوْمًا	a day		مَنْ رَبِّكُمْ	from your Lord
لَا تَجْزِى نَفْسٌ	when no one shall avail		عَظِيمٌ	great
عَنْ نَفْسٍ شَيْئًا	any one else at all		وَ إِذْ فَرَقْنَا	(50) And when We parted divided
وَّ لَا يُقْبَلُ	nor shall be accepted		بِكُمُ الْبَحْرَ	for you the sea
مِنْهَا	from one		فَأَنْجَيْنٰكُمْ	and We saved you
شَفَاعَةٌ	an intercession		وَ أَغْرَقْنَا	and We drowned
وَّ لَا يُؤْخَذُ	nor taken		الَ فِرْعَوْنَ	Pharaoh's people
مِنْهَا	from him / her		وَ أَنْتُمْ تَنْظُرُونَ	while you were looking
عَدْلٌ	a compensation			(before your eyes)
وَّ لَا هُمْ	nor will they be		وَ إِذْ	(51) And when
يُنْصَرُونَ	helped		وَعَدْنَا مُوسَى	We made an appointment with Mose
وَ إِذْ نَجَّيْنٰكُمْ	(49) And when We saved you		أَرْبَعِينَ	forty
مِنْ اٰلِ	from the people of		لَيْلَةً	nights
فِرْعَوْنَ	Pharaoh		ثُمَّ	then

اِتَّخَذْتُمُ	you took
اَلْعِجْلَ	the calf
مِنْ بَعْدِه	after him (in his absence)
وَ أَنْتُمْ ظٰلِمُونَ	and you were transgressors (unjust)
ثُمَّ عَفَوْنَا (52)	Then We pardoned
عَنْكُمْ	you
مِنْ بَعْدِ ذٰلِكَ	after that
لَعَلَّكُمْ	maybe you
تَشْكُرُونَ	give thanks
وَ إِذْ اٰتَيْنَا مُوسَى (53)	And when We gave Moses
اَلْكِتٰبَ	the Book
وَ الْفُرْقَانَ	and the criterion (of judgement)
لَعَلَّكُمْ	maybe you
تَهْتَدُونَ	become guided
وَ إِذْ قَالَ مُوسٰى (54)	And when Moses said
لِقَوْمِه	to his people
يٰقَوْمِ	O my people
إِنَّكُمْ	indeed you
ظَلَمْتُمْ	acted unjusty by
أَنْفُسَكُمْ	(against) yourselves
بِاتِّخَاذِكُمُ	by your taking (for worship)
اَلْعِجْلَ	the calf
فَتُوبُوا	so turn in repentance
إِلٰى بَارِئِكُمْ	to your Creator
فَاقْتُلُوا	so you kill
أَنْفُسَكُمْ	yourselves
ذٰلِكُمْ خَيْرٌ لَكُمْ	that is good for you
عِنْدَ بَارِئِكُمْ	according to your Creator
فَتَابَ عَلَيْكُمْ	so He will relent toward you

إِنَّهُ هُوَ	indeed He is
اَلتَّوَّابُ	Oft-Returning
اَلرَّحِيمُ	Most Merciful
وَ إِذْ قُلْتُمْ (55)	And when you said
يٰمُوسٰى	O Moses
لَنْ نُؤْمِنَ لَكَ	we shall never believe you
حَتّٰى	until
نَرَى اللهَ	we see Allah
جَهْرَةً	openly
فَأَخَذَتْكُمُ	whereupon took you
اَلصّٰعِقَةُ	the thunderbolt
وَ أَنْتُمْ تَنْظُرُونَ	while you were looking
ثُمَّ بَعَثْنٰكُمْ (56)	Again We brought you back to life
مِنْ بَعْدِ مَوْتِكُمْ	after your death
لَعَلَّكُمْ	maybe you
تَشْكُرُونَ	give thanks
وَ ظَلَّلْنَا عَلَيْكُمُ (57)	And we gave you the shade
اَلْغَمَامَ	(of) the clouds
وَ أَنْزَلْنَا	and We sent down
عَلَيْكُمُ	upon you
اَلْمَنَّ	the *manna*
وَ السَّلْوٰى	and the quail
كُلُوا	eat
مِنْ طَيِّبٰتِ	from good things
مَارَزَقْنٰكُمْ	that We provided you
وَمَا	and they did not
ظَلَمُونَا	do any harm to Us
وَ لٰكِنْ	but

كَانُوٓا أَنْفُسَهُمْ	they to themselves
يَظْلِمُونَ	harmed
وَ إِذْ قُلْنَا	(58) And when We said
ادْخُلُوا	enter
هٰذِهِ الْقَرْيَةَ	this town
فَكُلُوا مِنْهَا	so eat from it
حَيْثُ شِئْتُمْ	wherever you want
رَغَدًا	freely
وَّ ادْخُلُوا	and enter
الْبَابَ	the gate
سُجَّدًا	prostrating
وَّ قُولُوا حِطَّةً	and say "Repentance"
نَّغْفِرْ	We shall forgive
لَكُمْ	(for) you
خَطٰيٰكُمْ	your sins (mistakes)
وَسَنَزِيدُ	and We increase the reward of
الْمُحْسِنِينَ	those who do good
فَبَدَّلَ	(59) Then changed
الَّذِينَ	those who
ظَلَمُوا	acted unjustly
قَوْلاً	word (saying)
غَيْرَ	other
الَّذِى قِيلَ لَهُمْ	(than) what was said to them
فَأَنْزَلْنَا	so We sent down
عَلَى الَّذِينَ ظَلَمُوا	on those who acted unjustly
رِجْزًا	a torment
مِنَ السَّمَآءِ	from the heaven
بِمَا	because of (the fact that)
كَانُوا يَفْسُقُونَ	they use to act viciously/ disobediently

SECTION -7-

Sūrah Al-Baqarah
2: 60-61

THE TEXT OF THE QUR'ĀN

بِسْمِ اللّٰهِ الرَّحْمٰنِ الرَّحِيمِ

۞ وَإِذِ ٱسْتَسْقَىٰ مُوسَىٰ

لِقَوْمِهِ فَقُلْنَا ٱضْرِب بِّعَصَاكَ ٱلْحَجَرَ ۖ فَٱنفَجَرَتْ مِنْهُ

ٱثْنَتَا عَشْرَةَ عَيْنًا ۖ قَدْ عَلِمَ كُلُّ أُنَاسٍ مَّشْرَبَهُمْ ۖ كُلُوا

وَٱشْرَبُوا مِن رِّزْقِ ٱللّٰهِ وَلَا تَعْثَوْا فِي ٱلْأَرْضِ مُفْسِدِينَ ۝

وَإِذْ قُلْتُمْ يَٰمُوسَىٰ لَن نَّصْبِرَ عَلَىٰ طَعَامٍ وَٰحِدٍ فَٱدْعُ لَنَا رَبَّكَ

يُخْرِجْ لَنَا مِمَّا تُنۢبِتُ ٱلْأَرْضُ مِنۢ بَقْلِهَا وَقِثَّآئِهَا وَفُومِهَا

وَعَدَسِهَا وَبَصَلِهَا ۖ قَالَ أَتَسْتَبْدِلُونَ ٱلَّذِي هُوَ أَدْنَىٰ

بِٱلَّذِي هُوَ خَيْرٌ ۚ ٱهْبِطُوا مِصْرًا فَإِنَّ لَكُم مَّا سَأَلْتُمْ ۗ

وَضُرِبَتْ عَلَيْهِمُ ٱلذِّلَّةُ وَٱلْمَسْكَنَةُ وَبَآءُو بِغَضَبٍ مِّنَ

ٱللّٰهِ ۗ ذَٰلِكَ بِأَنَّهُمْ كَانُوا يَكْفُرُونَ بِـَٔايَٰتِ ٱللّٰهِ وَيَقْتُلُونَ

ٱلنَّبِيِّـۧنَ بِغَيْرِ ٱلْحَقِّ ۗ ذَٰلِكَ بِمَا عَصَوا وَّكَانُوا يَعْتَدُونَ ۝

TRANSLATIONS

Section 7: 60-61 (A. Y. Ali)

60. And remember Moses prayed for water for his people; We said: "Strike the rock with your

Section 7: 60-61 (M. M. Pickthall)

60. And when Moses asked for water for his people, We said: Smite {strike} with your staff." Then gushed forth therefrom twelve springs. Each group knew its own place for water. So eat and drink of the sustenance {life support} provided by Allāh. And do no evil nor mischief on the (face of the) earth.

61.　　　And remember you said: "O Moses! We cannot endure one kind of food (always); so beseech {plead, request} your Lord for us to produce for us of what the earth grows - its pot-herbs, and cucumbers, its garlic, lentils, and onions." He said: "Will you exchange the better for the worse? Go you down to any town, and you shall find what you want!" They were covered with humiliation and misery; they drew on themselves the wrath of Allāh. This because they went on rejecting the Signs of Allāh and slaying His Messengers without just cause. This because they rebelled and went on transgressing {violating}.

staff the rock. And there gushed out therefrom twelve springs (so that) each tribe knew their drinking place. Eat and drink of that which Allāh has provided, and do not act corruptly, making mischief in the earth.

61.　　　And when you said: O Moses! We are weary of one kind of food; so call upon your Lord for us that he bring forth for us of that which the earth grows of its herbs and its cucumbers and its corn and its lentils and its onions. He said: Would you exchange that which is higher for that which is lower? Go down to settled country; thus, you shall get that which you demand. And humiliation and wretchedness {misery} were stamped upon them and they were visited with wrath from Allāh. That was because they disbelieved in Allāh's revelations and slew the prophets wrongfully. That was for their disobedience and transgression.

EXPLANATION

60:　　　Here, we have a reference to the tribal organization of the Jews, which played a great part in their forty years' march through the Arabian deserts (Num: 1-2) and their subsequent settlement in the land of Canaan (Josh: 13-14). The twelve tribes were descended from the sons of Jacob, whose title was Israel (Soldier of God). The fixed stations and watering places in camp, and fixed territorial areas later in the Promised Land prevented confusion and mutual jealousies.

61:　　　The word *Misr* may mean any town, or the Egypt of Pharaoh. Note a subtle reminiscence as well as a severe reproach. The rebellious children of Israel murmured at the blandness of the food they were blessed with in the desert. They were evidently craving after the delicacies of the Egypt they had left behind. Moses's reproach to them was twofold: Ahead is the rich Promised Land, which you are reluctant to march to; behind is Egypt, the land of bondage. Which is better? Would you exchange the better for the worse? After they got to the Promised Land, they continued to rebel against God. They were punished and humiliated, eventually suffering a national disaster dispersing them all over the earth.

IMPORTANT POINTS TO LEARN AND REFLECT UPON

- Allāh favored Banī Isrā'īl by granting each tribe a separate spring of fresh water and providing the food through *Manna* and *Salwa*.

- Banī Isrā'īl continued to complain and later continued to disobey and were punished.

- Allāh has shown many favors to the Muslim *Ummah*. Muslims must obey Allāh and follow the *Sunnah* of His Messenger.

ARABIC GLOSSARY WORDS

بِسْمِ اللهِ الرَّحْمٰنِ الرَّحِيمِ

وَ إِذْ (60)	And when	يُخْرِجْ لَنَا	(so that) He brings out for us
اسْتَسْقٰى مُوسٰى	Moses prayed for water	مِمَّا تُنْبِتُ آلْأَرْضُ	(from) whatever grows on the earth
لِقَوْمِهِ	for his people	مِنْ بَقْلِهَا	of its vegetables (or green herbs)
فَقُلْنَا	so We said	وَقِثَّائِهَا	and its cucumbers
اضْرِبْ	strike (O'Moses)	وَفُومِهَا	and its garlic
بِعَصَاكَ	with your staff	وَعَدَسِهَا	and its lentils
الْحَجَرَ	the stone (the rock)	وَبَصَلِهَا	and its onions
فَانْفَجَرَتْ	so gushed forth	قَالَ أَتَسْتَبْدِلُونَ	he said are you exchanging
مِنْهُ	from it	آلَّذِى هُوَ	that which is
اثْنَتَا عَشْرَةَ	twelve	أَدْنٰى	worse
عَيْنًا	spring(s)	بِالَّذِى هُوَ	with that which is
قَدْ عَلِمَ	knew	خَيْرٌ	better
كُلُّ أُنَاسٍ	each people (each tribe)	آهْبِطُوا	you go down to
مَشْرَبَهُمْ	their drinking place	مِصْرًا	(any) town
كُلُوا وَ اشْرَبُوا	eat and drink	فَإِنَّ لَكُمْ	surely you shall have
مِنْ رِزْقِ اللهِ	from the provisions of Allah	مَّا سَأَلْتُمْ	what you are asking for
وَ لاَ تَعْثَوْا	and do not transgress	وَضُرِبَتْ عَلَيْهِمُ	and they were covered with
فِى الْأَرْضِ	in the earth	الذِّلَّةُ	humiliation
مُفْسِدِينَ	creating corruption	وَ الْمَسْكَنَةُ	and misery
	(lit. acting as corrupt people)	وَ بَآءُو	and they drew themselves
وَ إِذْ قُلْتُمْ (61)	And when you said	بِغَضَبٍ	(with) the wrath
يٰمُوسٰى	O Moses	مِّنَ اللهِ	from Allah
لَنْ نَصْبِرَ	we will never stand (are weary of)	ذٰلِكَ	this is because
عَلٰى طَعَامٍ وَّاحِدٍ	(on) one kind of food	بِأَنَّهُمْ	infact-they
فَادْعُ لَنَا رَبَّكَ	so you pray for us to your Lord	كَانُوا يَكْفُرُونَ	(they) use to reject

بِاٰیٰتِ اللهِ	the Signs of Allah	ذٰلِكَ	that was
وَ یَقْتُلُونَ	and used to kill	بِمَا عَصَوا	because they used to rebel
النَّبِیِّینَ	the Prophets	وَّ كَانُوا یَعْتَدُونَ	and used to transgress
بِغَیْرِ الْحَقِّ	without just a cause		

SECTION -8-

Sūrah Al-Baqarah

2: 62-71

THE TEXT OF THE QUR'ĀN

بِسْمِ اللّٰهِ الرَّحْمٰنِ الرَّحِيمِ

إِنَّ الَّذِينَ ءَامَنُوا وَالَّذِينَ هَادُوا وَالنَّصَارَىٰ وَالصَّابِئِينَ مَنْ ءَامَنَ بِاللّٰهِ وَالْيَوْمِ الْأَخِرِ وَعَمِلَ صَالِحًا فَلَهُمْ أَجْرُهُمْ عِندَ رَبِّهِمْ وَلَا خَوْفٌ عَلَيْهِمْ وَلَا هُمْ يَحْزَنُونَ ۝ وَإِذْ أَخَذْنَا مِيثَاقَكُمْ وَرَفَعْنَا فَوْقَكُمُ الطُّورَ خُذُوا مَا ءَاتَيْنَاكُم بِقُوَّةٍ وَاذْكُرُوا مَا فِيهِ لَعَلَّكُمْ تَتَّقُونَ ۝ ثُمَّ تَوَلَّيْتُم مِّنۢ بَعْدِ ذَٰلِكَ فَلَوْلَا فَضْلُ اللّٰهِ عَلَيْكُمْ وَرَحْمَتُهُۥ لَكُنتُم مِّنَ الْخَاسِرِينَ ۝ وَلَقَدْ عَلِمْتُمُ الَّذِينَ اعْتَدَوْا مِنكُمْ فِي السَّبْتِ فَقُلْنَا لَهُمْ كُونُوا قِرَدَةً خَاسِئِينَ ۝ فَجَعَلْنَاهَا نَكَالًا لِّمَا بَيْنَ يَدَيْهَا وَمَا خَلْفَهَا وَمَوْعِظَةً لِّلْمُتَّقِينَ ۝ وَإِذْ قَالَ مُوسَىٰ لِقَوْمِهِۦ إِنَّ اللّٰهَ يَأْمُرُكُمْ أَن تَذْبَحُوا بَقَرَةً قَالُوا أَتَتَّخِذُنَا هُزُوًا قَالَ أَعُوذُ بِاللّٰهِ أَنْ أَكُونَ مِنَ الْجَاهِلِينَ ۝ قَالُوا ادْعُ لَنَا رَبَّكَ يُبَيِّن لَّنَا مَا هِيَ قَالَ إِنَّهُۥ يَقُولُ إِنَّهَا بَقَرَةٌ لَّا فَارِضٌ وَلَا بِكْرٌ عَوَانٌۢ بَيْنَ ذَٰلِكَ فَافْعَلُوا مَا تُؤْمَرُونَ ۝

قَالُوا ادْعُ لَنَا رَبَّكَ يُبَيِّن لَّنَا مَا لَوْنُهَا قَالَ إِنَّهُ يَقُولُ إِنَّهَا بَقَرَةٌ صَفْرَاءُ فَاقِعٌ لَّوْنُهَا تَسُرُّ النَّاظِرِينَ ۝

قَالُوا ادْعُ لَنَا رَبَّكَ يُبَيِّن لَّنَا مَا هِىَ إِنَّ الْبَقَرَ تَشَبَهَ عَلَيْنَا وَإِنَّا إِن شَاءَ اللَّهُ لَمُهْتَدُونَ ۝ قَالَ إِنَّهُ يَقُولُ إِنَّهَا بَقَرَةٌ لَّا ذَلُولٌ تُثِيرُ الْأَرْضَ وَلَا تَسْقِى الْحَرْثَ مُسَلَّمَةٌ لَّا شِيَةَ فِيهَا قَالُوا الْـَٔنَ جِئْتَ بِالْحَقِّ فَذَبَحُوهَا وَمَا كَادُوا يَفْعَلُونَ ۝

TRANSLATIONS

Section 8: 62-71 (A. Y. Ali)

62. Those who believe (in the Qur'ān), and those who follow the Jewish (scriptures), and the Christians and the Sabians - and who believe in Allāh and the Last Day and work righteousness, shall have their reward with their Lord; on them, shall be no fear, nor shall they grieve.

63. And remember, We took your Covenant, and We raised above you (the towering height) of Mount (Sinai) (saying): "Hold firmly to what We have given you and bring (ever) to remembrance what is therein: perchance {perhaps?} You may fear Allāh."

64. But you turned back thereafter; had it not been for the Grace and Mercy of Allāh to you, you had surely been among the lost.

65. And well you knew those amongst you who transgressed in the matter of the Sabbath; We said to them: "Be you apes, despised and rejected."

66. So We made it an example to their own time and to their posterity {offspring, descendants} and a lesson to those who fear Allāh {have *Taqwā*}

Section 8: 62-71 (M. M. Pickthall)

62. Lo! Those who believe (in that which is revealed unto you, Muḥammad), and those who are Jews, and Christians, and Sabaeans - whoever believes in Allāh and the Last Day and does right - surely, their reward is with their Lord, and there shall no fear come upon them neither shall they grieve.

63. And (remember, O children of Israel) when We made a covenant with you and caused the Mount to tower above you, (saying): Hold fast that which We have given you, and remember that which is therein, that you may ward off (evil).

64. Then, even after that, you turned away, and if it had not been for the grace of Allāh and His mercy, you had been among the losers.

65. And you know of those of you who broke the Sabbath, bow We said unto them: Be you apes, despised and hated!

66. And We made it an example to their own and to succeeding generations, and an admonition {lesson} to the God-fearing.

67.	And remember, Moses said to his people: "Allāh commands that you sacrifice a heifer {cow}" They said: "You make a laughingstock of us?" He said: "Allāh save me from being an ignorant (fool)!"	67.	And when Moses said unto his people: Lo! Allah commands you that you sacrifice a cow, they said: Do you make game of us? He answered: Allāh forbid that I should be among the foolish!
68.	They said: "Beseech on our behalf your Lord to make plain {clear} to us what (heifer) it is!" He said: "He said: "The heifer should be neither too old nor too young, but of middling age: now do what you are commanded!"	68.	They said: Pray for us unto your Lord that He make clear to us what (cow) she is. (Moses) answered: Lo! He says, Verily, she is a cow neither with calf nor immature; (she is) between the two conditions; so do that which you are commanded.
69.	They said: "Beseech on our behalf your Lord to make plain {clear} to us her color." He said: "He says: a fawn-colored {yellow} heifer, pure and rich in tone, the admiration of {pleasing to} beholders!"	69.	They said: Pray for us unto your Lord that He make clear to us of what color she is. (Moses) answered: Lo! He says: Verily, she is a yellow cow. Bright is her color, gladdening beholders.
70.	They said: "Beseech on our behalf your Lord to make plain {clear} to us what she is: to us are all heifers alike: we wish indeed for guidance if Allāh wills."	70.	They said: Pray for us unto your Lord that He make clear to us what (cow) she is. Lo! Cows are much alike to us; and Lo! If Allāh wills, we may be led aright.
71.	He said: "He says: a heifer not trained to till the soil or water the fields; sound and without blemish {defect}" They said: "Now have you brought the truth." Then they offered her in sacrifice, but not with goodwill.	71.	(Moses) answered: Lo! He says: Verily, she is a cow unyoked; she ploughs not the soil nor waters the tilth; whole and without mark. They said: Now, you bring the truth. So they sacrificed her, though almost they did not.

EXPLANATION

62: {Sabeans were a little-known ancient religious sect. The Qur'ān recognizes them as People of the Book. AG} The latest research has revealed a small remnant of a religious community of about 2,000 in Lower Iraq, near Basrah. They believed in theories of Darkness and Light, as in Zoroastrianism. They lived in peace and harmony among their Muslim neighbors. They resemble the *Sabi'ūn* mentioned in the Qur'ān, but we cannot be sure they the same. See 2:38, where the same phrase occurs. It recurs over and over afterwards. The point of the verse is that Islām does not teach an exclusive doctrine, and is not meant exclusively for one people. The Jews claim this for themselves, and the Christians cling to the idea of Vicarious Atonement. The attitude of Islām is entirely different. Islām existed before the preaching of Prophet Muhammad ﷺ on this earth, and its teaching (submission to God's will) has been and will be the teaching of every true religion for all times, and for all peoples.

63: The Mountain of Sinai (*Tur as-Sinin*) is a prominent mountain in the Arabian desert, in the peninsula between the two arms of the Red Sea. Here, the Ten Commandments and the Law were given to Moses. Hence, it is now called the Mountain of Moses (*Jabal Musa*). The Israelites encamped at the foot of it for nearly a year. It is there that they entered into their Covenant with God (Exod 19: 5,8,16,18).

64: {The Israelites broke the Covenants too frequently, but God forgave them repeatedly and gave them fresh chances. The coming of Prophet Jesus ﷺ and Prophet Muhammad ﷺ gave them a new opportunity to repent and respond to the New Covenant of Jesus ﷺ and the Final Covenant of Prophet Muhammad ﷺ . AG}

65: The punishment for breach of the Sabbath under Mosaic law was death. There must have been a Jewish tradition about a whole fishing community in a seaside town. This community persisted in breaking the Sabbath, and its inhabitants were turned into apes, (see Al-A'raf 7:163-166). Or should we translate in both these passages as, "Be as apes", instead of "Be apes"?

66: {The severe Divine judgment against the Jews for breaking His Law was to serve as an example for all people, including Muslims and of for all times; we are warned that the disobedience of God's commandments brings his severe Judgment. AG}

67-71: This story or parable of the heifer in 2:67-71 should be read with the parable of the dead man brought to life in 2:72-73. The stories were accepted in Jewish traditions, which are themselves based on certain sacrificial directions in the Old Testament (see Num 19:1-10). Moses announced the sacrifice to the Israelites, and they treated it as a jest, putting it off on one pretext and another. When at last they were driven into a corner, they made the sacrifice, but their hearts weren't in it. A sincere sacrifice in obedience to Divine Commandment would have made it acceptable for the purification of their sins.

IMPORTANT POINTS TO LEARN AND REFLECT UPON

- Whoever does a good deed is rewarded by Allāh ﷻ for it.

- When Allāh ﷻ asks us to do something, we must do it without questioning or complaining

- To follow any command of Allāh ﷻ, with reluctance and reservation is as if not following it at all.

ARABIC GLOSSARY WORDS

بِسْمِ اللهِ الرَّحْمٰنِ الرَّحِيمِ

(62) Indeed those who	إِنَّ الَّذِينَ	and neither will be any fear	وَ لَا خَوْفٌ
believe	اٰمَنُوا	on (for) them	عَلَيْهِمْ
and those who	وَ الَّذِينَ	nor shall they	وَ لَا هُمْ
became Jew	هَادُوا	have any worry	يَحْزَنُونَ
and the Christians	وَ النَّصٰرٰى	(63) And when	وَ إِذْ
and the Sabians	وَ الصّٰبِئِينَ	We took	أَخَذْنَا
whoever believed	مَنْ اٰمَنَ	your covenant	مِيثَاقَكُمْ
in Allah	بِاللهِ	and We raised	وَرَفَعْنَا
and the Last Day	وَ الْيَوْمِ الْاٰخِرِ	above you	فَوْقَكُمُ
and did	وَعَمِلَ	the Mount Sinai	الطُّورَ
good (deeds)	صَالِحًا	hold what	خُذُوا مَآ
so for them (there is)	فَلَهُمْ	We gave you	اٰتَيْنٰكُمْ
their reward	أَجْرُهُمْ	with strength (firmly)	بِقُوَّةٍ
with their Lord	عِنْدَ رَبِّهِمْ	and remember	وَّ اذْكُرُوا

مَا فِيهِ	what is in it	إِنَّ اللهَ	indeed Allah
لَعَلَّكُمْ تَتَّقُونَ	so that you learn piety	يَأْمُرُكُمْ	commands you
(64) ثُمَّ	Then	أَنْ تَذْبَحُوا	that you slaughter
تَوَلَّيْتُمْ	you turned away	بَقَرَةً	a cow
مِنْ بَعْدِ ذٰلِكَ	after that	قَالُوا	they said
فَلَوْلَا	so had there not been	أَتَتَّخِذُنَا هُزُوًا	are you jesting with us?
فَضْلُ اللهِ	(special) Favor of Allah	قَالَ	he said
عَلَيْكُمْ	on you	أَعُوذُ بِاللهِ	I seek refuge with Allah
وَرَحْمَتُهُ	and His Mercy	أَنْ أَكُونَ	that I am
لَكُنْتُمْ	you would have been	مِنَ الْجَاهِلِينَ	among the ignorant
مِنَ الْخَاسِرِينَ	among the losers	(68) قَالُوا	They said
(65) وَ لَقَدْ	And indeed	اُدْعُ لَنَا	pray for us
عَلِمْتُمُ	you knew	رَبَّكَ	(to) your Lord
الَّذِينَ	those who	يُبَيِّن لَنَا	(that) He makes clear for us
اعْتَدَوْا	transgressed	مَا هِىَ	what she is
مِنْكُمْ	among you	قَالَ	he said
فِى السَّبْتِ	in (concerning) the Sabbath	إِنَّهُ يَقُولُ	He says
فَقُلْنَا	so We said	إِنَّهَا	it is
لَهُمْ	to them	بَقَرَةٌ	a cow
كُونُوا قِرَدَةً	be apes	لَا فَارِضٌ	neither a worn out cow
خَاسِئِينَ	despised ones	وَ لَا بِكْرٌ	nor a heifer
(66) فَجَعَلْنَاهَا	So We made it	عَوَانٌ	(of) middle age
نَكَالاً	an examplary punishment	بَيْنَ ذٰلِكَ	between that
لِّمَا بَيْنَ يَدَيْهَا	for its time (what was in front of it)	فَافْعَلُوا	so do
وَمَا خَلْفَهَا	and for the times to come	مَا تُؤْمَرُونَ	what you are commanded
وَمَوْعِظَةً	and a warning	(69) قَالُوا	They said
لِّلْمُتَّقِينَ	for the *muttaqis* (Godfearing)	اُدْعُ لَنَا	pray for us
(67) وَ إِذْ قَالَ مُوسَى	And when Moses said	رَبَّكَ	(to) your Lord
لِقَوْمِهِ	to his people	يُبَيِّن لَنَا	(that) He makes clear for us

مَا لَوْنُهَا	what her color is
قَالَ	he said
إِنَّهُ يَقُولُ	He says
إِنَّهَا	it is
بَقَرَةٌ	a cow
صَفْرَاءُ	yellow
فَاقِعٌ لَوْنُهَا	her bright color
تَسُرُّ	pleasing
النَّظِرِينَ	the beholders
(70) قَالُوا	They said
أُدْعُ لَنَا رَبَّكَ	pray for us (to) your Lord
يُبَيِّنْ	(that) He makes clear
لَنَا	for us
مَا هِىَ	what she is
إِنَّ الْبَقَرَ	indeed the cows
تَشَبَّهَ عَلَيْنَا	seem all alike to us
وَإِنَّا	and we,
إِنْ شَاءَ اللهُ	if Allah wills

لَمُهْتَدُونَ	shall be guided (choose the right cow)
(71) قَالَ إِنَّهُ	He (Moses) said
يَقُولُ	He says
إِنَّهَا بَقَرَةٌ	it should be a cow
لَا ذَلُولٌ	unyoked
تُثِيرُ الْأَرْضَ	neither ploughs the earth
وَ لَا تَسْقِى	nor waters
الْحَرْثَ مُسَلَّمَةٌ	the fields (tilth) free of faults
لَا شِيَةَ	no defect
فِيهَا	in her
قَالُوا	they said
الْئَنَ	now
جِئْتَ بِالْحَقِّ	you brought the truth (correct information)
فَذَبَحُوهَا	so they slaughtered her
وَمَا كَادُوا يَفْعَلُونَ	and they were not inclined to do it

SECTION -9-

Sūrah Al-Baqarah
2: 72-82

THE TEXT OF THE QUR'ĀN

بِسْمِ اللّٰهِ الرَّحْمٰنِ الرَّحِيمِ

وَإِذْ

قَتَلْتُمْ نَفْسًا فَادَّارَءْتُمْ فِيهَا ۖ وَاللّٰهُ مُخْرِجٌ مَّا كُنْتُمْ تَكْتُمُونَ ۝

فَقُلْنَا اضْرِبُوهُ بِبَعْضِهَا ۚ كَذٰلِكَ يُحْيِ اللّٰهُ الْمَوْتٰى وَيُرِيكُمْ ءَايٰتِهِ لَعَلَّكُمْ تَعْقِلُونَ ۝ ثُمَّ قَسَتْ قُلُوبُكُمْ مِّنْ بَعْدِ ذٰلِكَ فَهِىَ كَالْحِجَارَةِ أَوْ أَشَدُّ قَسْوَةً ۚ وَإِنَّ مِنَ الْحِجَارَةِ لَمَا يَتَفَجَّرُ مِنْهُ الْأَنْهَارُ ۚ وَإِنَّ مِنْهَا لَمَا يَشَّقَّقُ فَيَخْرُجُ مِنْهُ الْمَاءُ ۚ وَإِنَّ مِنْهَا لَمَا يَهْبِطُ مِنْ خَشْيَةِ اللّٰهِ ۗ وَمَا اللّٰهُ بِغٰفِلٍ عَمَّا تَعْمَلُونَ ۝

أَفَتَطْمَعُونَ أَنْ يُؤْمِنُوا لَكُمْ وَقَدْ كَانَ فَرِيقٌ مِّنْهُمْ يَسْمَعُونَ كَلٰمَ اللّٰهِ ثُمَّ يُحَرِّفُونَهُ مِنْ بَعْدِ مَا عَقَلُوهُ وَهُمْ يَعْلَمُونَ ۝ وَإِذَا لَقُوا الَّذِينَ ءَامَنُوا قَالُوا ءَامَنَّا وَإِذَا خَلَا بَعْضُهُمْ إِلٰى بَعْضٍ قَالُوا أَتُحَدِّثُونَهُمْ بِمَا فَتَحَ اللّٰهُ عَلَيْكُمْ لِيُحَاجُّوكُمْ بِهِ عِنْدَ رَبِّكُمْ ۚ أَفَلَا تَعْقِلُونَ ۝

أَوَلَا يَعْلَمُونَ أَنَّ اللّٰهَ يَعْلَمُ مَا يُسِرُّونَ وَمَا يُعْلِنُونَ ۝

وَمِنْهُمْ أُمِّيُّونَ لَا يَعْلَمُونَ ٱلْكِتَبَ إِلَّا أَمَانِيَّ وَإِنْ هُمْ

إِلَّا يَظُنُّونَ ۝ فَوَيْلٌ لِّلَّذِينَ يَكْتُبُونَ ٱلْكِتَبَ بِأَيْدِيهِمْ

ثُمَّ يَقُولُونَ هَذَا مِنْ عِندِ ٱللَّهِ لِيَشْتَرُوا بِهِ ثَمَنًا قَلِيلًا

فَوَيْلٌ لَّهُم مِّمَّا كَتَبَتْ أَيْدِيهِمْ وَوَيْلٌ لَّهُم مِّمَّا يَكْسِبُونَ

۝ وَقَالُوا لَن تَمَسَّنَا ٱلنَّارُ إِلَّا أَيَّامًا مَّعْدُودَةً قُلْ

أَتَّخَذْتُمْ عِندَ ٱللَّهِ عَهْدًا فَلَن يُخْلِفَ ٱللَّهُ عَهْدَهُ أَمْ تَقُولُونَ

عَلَى ٱللَّهِ مَا لَا تَعْلَمُونَ ۝ بَلَى مَنْ كَسَبَ سَيِّئَةً

وَأَحَاطَتْ بِهِ خَطِيئَتُهُ فَأُوْلَئِكَ أَصْحَبُ ٱلنَّارِ هُمْ

فِيهَا خَلِدُونَ ۝ وَٱلَّذِينَ ءَامَنُوا وَعَمِلُوا ٱلصَّلِحَتِ

أُوْلَئِكَ أَصْحَبُ ٱلْجَنَّةِ هُمْ فِيهَا خَلِدُونَ ۝

TRANSLATIONS

Section 9: 72-82 (A. Y. Ali)

Section 9: 72-82 (M. M. Pickthall)

72.   Remember, you slew a man and fell into a dispute among yourselves as to the crime: but Allāh was to bring forth what you did hide.

73.   So We said: "Strike the (body) with a piece of the (heifer)." Thus, Allāh brings the dead to life and shows you His Signs: perchance, you may understand.

74.   Thenceforth were your hearts hardened; they became like a rock and even worse in hardness. For among rocks, there are some from which rivers gush forth; others there are which when split asunder send forth water; and others which sink for fear of Allāh. And Allāh is not unmindful of what you do.

72.   And (remember) when you slew a man and disagreed concerning it and Allāh brought forth that which you were hiding.

73.   And We said: Smite him with some of it. Thus, Allāh brings the dead to life and shows you His Portents {signs} so that you may understand.

74.   Then, even after that, your hearts were hardened and became as rocks, or worse than rocks, for hardness. For indeed, there are rocks from out which rivers gush, and indeed, there are rocks which split asunder so that water flows from them. And indeed, there are rocks which fall down for the

75.   Can you (O you men of Faith) entertain the hope that they will believe in you? - Seeing that a party of them heard the word of Allāh, and perverted {twisted} it knowingly after they understood it.

76.   Behold! When they meet the men of Faith, they say: "We believe": but when they meet each other in private, they say: "Shall you tell them what Allāh has revealed to you, that they may engage you in argument about it before your Lord?" - Do you not understand (their aim)?

77.   Know they not that Allāh knows what they conceal and what they reveal?

78.   And there are among them illiterates, who know not the Book, but (see therein their own) desires, and they do nothing but conjecture {guess}

79.   Then woe to those who write the Book with their own hands, and then say: "This is from Allāh," to traffic with it for a miserable price - Woe to them for what their hands do write, and for the gain they make thereby.

80.   And they say: "The Fire shall not touch us but for a few numbered days;" Say: "Have you taken a promise from Allāh, for He never breaks His promise? Or is it that you say of Allāh what you do not know?"

81.   Indeed, those who seek gain in Evil, and are girt round {surrounded) by their sins - they are Companions of the Fire: therein shall they abide (forever).

82.   But those who have faith and work righteousness. They are Companions of the Garden: therein shall they abide (forever).

fear of Allāh. Allāh is not unaware of what you do.

75.   Have you any hope that they will be true to you when a party of them used to listen to the Word of Allāh, then used to change it, after they had understood it, knowingly?

76.   And when they fall in with those who believe, they say: We believe. But when they go apart one with another they say: Tell them of that which Allāh has disclosed to you that they may contend with you before your Lord concerning it? Have you then no sense?

77.   Are they then unaware that Allāh knows that which they keep hidden and that which they proclaim?

78.   Among them are unlettered {illiterate} folk who know the scripture not except from hearsay {rumor}. They but guess.

79.   Therefore, woe be unto those who write the Scripture with their hands and then say, "This is from Allāh," that they may purchase a small gain therewith. Woe unto them for that their hands have written, and woe unto them for that they earn thereby.

80.   And they say: The Fire (of punishment) will not touch us but for a certain number of days. Say: Have you received a covenant from Allāh - truly Allāh will not break His covenant--or tell you concerning Allāh that which you know not?

81.   Surely, but whosoever has done evil and his sin surrounds him; such are rightful owners of the Fire; they will abide therein.

82.   And those who believe and do good works: such are rightful owners of the Garden. They will abide therein.

EXPLANATION

72-73:   According to Jewish account, in a certain case of murder, everyone tried to clear himself of guilt and lay the blame at the door of others. And this after they tried to make excuses and prevent the heifer from being slain, as in the last story. A portion of the sacrificed heifer was ordered to be placed on the corpse, which came to life and disclosed the whole story of the crime. The lesson of this parable is that people may try to hide their crimes, but Allāh ﷻ will bring them to light in unexpected ways.

74:    The sinner's heart gets harder and harder. It is even harder than rocks, of which a beautiful poetic allegory is placed before us. There are rocks that weep voluntarily, like repentant hearts. Then, there are rocks which have to be split, and underneath, we find abundant waters. Such are the hearts of a less degree of fineness, which melt into tears when some great blow or calamity falls. And lastly, there are the rocks which slip or sink by geological pressure or in an earthquake, and send forth large spouts of water. So, there are hearts which will come to God by no higher motive than fear. But the hardened sinner is worse than all these hardened rocks.

75-76: The immediate argument applies to the Jews of Madīnah, but the more general argument applies to the people of Faith, and the people without Faith. In Deut. 18:18 God informs Moses: "I will raise them up a prophet from among their brethren, like unto you." Which was interpreted by some of their scholars as referring to Prophet Muḥammad ﷺ ; understanding this, they came to accept Islam. The Arabs are a kindred branch of the Semitic family and are correctly described in relation to the Jews as "their brethren". There is no question that there was not another prophet "like unto Moses" until Prophet Muḥammad ﷺ came. In fact, the postscript of Deuteronomy, which was written many centuries after Moses, says: "There arose not a prophet since in Israel like unto Moses, whom the Lord knew face to face." But the Jews were jealous of Prophet Muḥammad ﷺ, and played a double part. When the Muslim community began to grow stronger, they pretended to be allies with them. In reality, however, they tried to withhold any knowledge of their own Scriptures from the Muslims, in case they should be beaten by their own arguments. The more general interpretation holds good in all ages. Belief and disbelief are pitted against each other. Belief has to struggle against power, position, organization, and privilege. When it gains ground, disbelief comes forward insincerely and claims fellowship. But in its own mind, it is jealous of the authentic revealed knowledge which belief brings into the service of Allāh ﷻ.

77: {Allāh ﷻ, however, is well aware of their designs and shall defeat them in the end. AG}

78: The Jews wanted to withhold knowledge, but what knowledge did they have? Many of them, even if they could read, were no better than illiterates, for they knew not their own true Scriptures and read into them what they wanted. Perhaps, this brought them profit, but it did not bring them guidance.

79: {"Writing with their own hands" means inventing books themselves and inserting their own ideas into revelation. Modern literary criticism of the Bible (in its many versions) bears out this Qur'ānic testimony of 1400 years ago (See the pioneering work of Harvard scholar Richard E. Friedman; "Who Wrote the Bible?", Perennial Library, 1988). AG}

80: The Jews might say: Whatever the terror of Hell may be for other people, our sins will be forgiven, because we are the children of Abraham {Ibrāhim}; at worst, we shall suffer a short definite punishment, (Read this verse with *Al-Baqarah* 2:81-82). The general application is also clear. If disbelief claims some special benefit now, such as race, civilization, political power, and so on, it will not avail in Allāh's ﷻ sight. His promise is sure, but His promise is for those who seek Him in Faith, and show it in their righteous conduct.

81-82: This is many degrees worse than merely falling into evil: it is going out to "earn evil". Due punishment to Evildoers and reward for the righteous awaits in the Hereafter.

IMPORTANT POINTS TO LEARN AND REFLECT UPON

- The disobedience to Allāh ﷻ makes our hearts harder than stones

- For anyone who intentionally changes the words or meanings of Allāh's ﷻ revelation is a grave punishment

- Allāh ﷻ punishes and rewards people according to their deeds and not according to their race or tribe.

ARABIC GLOSSARY WORDS

بِسْمِ اللهِ الرَّحْمٰنِ الرَّحِيمِ

(72) وَ إِذْ	And remember when	اَلْأَنْهٰرُ	the rivers
قَتَلْتُمْ	you killed	وَإِنَّ	and indeed
نَفْسًا	a person	مِنْهَا	among them (rocks)
فَادّٰرَءْتُمْ	then you disputed	لَمَا يَشَّقَّقُ	there are such that split open
فِيهَا	in it	فَيَخْرُجُ	so comes out
وَ اللهُ مُخْرِجٌ	and Allah was to bring forth	مِنْهُ	from it
مَّا كُنْتُمْ تَكْتُمُونَ	what you were hiding	اَلْمَآءُ	the water
(73) فَقُلْنَا	So We said	وَ إِنَّ مِنْهَا	and indeed among them
اضْرِبُوهُ	strike him	لَمَا يَهْبِطُ	there are such that fall down
بِبَعْضِهَا	with some (part) of her	مِنْ خَشْيَةِ اللهِ	due to the fear of Allah
كَذٰلِكَ	like this (this is the way)	وَمَا اللهُ بِغَافِلٍ	and Allah is not unaware
يُحْىِ اللهُ	Allah brings to life	عَمَّا تَعْمَلُونَ	of what you are doing
الْمَوْتٰى	the dead	(75) أَفَتَطْمَعُونَ	Are you keen (lit.greedy)
وَ يُرِيكُمْ	and shows you	أَنْ يُؤْمِنُوا لَكُمْ	thay they believe with you
ٰايٰتِهِ	His signs	وَ قَدْ كَانَ	and indeed there has been
لَعَلَّكُمْ تَعْقِلُونَ	so that you may understand	فَرِيقٌ	a party (group)
(74) ثُمَّ قَسَتْ	Then hardened	مِنْهُمْ	among them
قُلُوبُكُمْ	your hearts	يَسْمَعُونَ	who (used to) listen
مِنْ بَعْدِ ذٰلِكَ	after that	كَلٰمَ اللهِ	Allah's word(s)
فَهِىَ	so they (hearts)	ثُمَّ	and then
كَالْحِجَارَةِ	(became) like the stones (rocks)	يُحَرِّفُونَهُ	they (used to) twist it
أَوْ أَشَدُّ قَسْوَةً	or even harder	مِنْ بَعْدِ مَا	after that
وَإِنَّ	and indeed there are	عَقَلُوهُ	they understood it
مِنَ الْحِجَارَةِ	among the rocks	وَهُمْ يَعْلَمُونَ	and they know
لَمَا يَتَفَجَّرُ	(such) that gush forth	(76) وَ إِذَا	And when
مِنْهُ	from it	لَقُوا	they meet

الَّذِينَ اٰمَنُوا	those who believe
قَالُوا اٰمَنَّا	they say we believe
وَ إِذَا	and when
خَلَا	meet in private
بَعْضُهُمْ إِلَىٰ بَعْض	with each other
قَالُوا	they say
أَتُحَدِّثُونَهُمْ	do you tell them
بِمَا فَتَحَ اللهُ	what Allah revealed
عَلَيْكُمْ	upon you
لِيُحَاجُّوكُمْ	so that they argue (you)
بِهِ	with it
عِنْدَ رَبِّكُمْ	before your Lord
أَفَلَا	do not
تَعْقِلُونَ	you understand
أَوَ لَا يَعْلَمُونَ	(77) And do they not know
أَنَّ	(that) indeed
اللهُ يَعْلَمُ	Allah knows
مَا يُسِرُّونَ	what they keep secret
وَمَا يُعْلِنُونَ	and what they announce
وَ مِنْهُمْ	(78) And among them
أُمِّيُّونَ	(are) illiterates
لَا يَعْلَمُونَ	they do not know
الْكِتٰبَ	the Book
إِلَّا أَمَانِيَّ	except from their fancies
وَ إِنْ هُمْ	and they (do) nothing
إِلَّا يَظُنُّونَ	but conjecture
فَوَيْلٌ	(79) So woe
لَلَّذِينَ	to those who
يَكْتُبُونَ	write
الْكِتٰبَ	the Book
بِأَيْدِيهِمْ	with their (own) hands
ثُمَّ يَقُولُونَ	then they say
هٰذَا مِنْ عِنْدِ الله	this is from Allah
لِيَشْتَرُوا بِهِ	in order to buy (sell) with it
ثَمَنًا قَلِيلًا	a little price
فَوَيْلٌ لَهُمْ	so woe to them
مِمَّا كَتَبَتْ	for whatever wrote
أَيْدِيهِمْ	their hands
وَوَيْلٌ لَهُمْ	and woe to them
مِمَّا يَكْسِبُونَ	for whatever they earned
(80) وَقَالُوا	And they say
لَنْ تَمَسَّنَا النَّارُ	the Fire will never touch us
إِلَّا أَيَّامًا مَعْدُودَةً	except a few days.
قُلْ	say
أَتَّخَذْتُمْ	have you taken
عِنْدَ الله عَهْدًا	a covenant with God
فَلَنْ يُخْلِفَ الله	so Allah will never break
عَهْدَهُ	His covenant
أَمْ تَقُولُونَ	or you say
عَلَى الله	concerning (against) Allah
مَا لَا تَعْلَمُونَ	what you do not know
(81) بَلَىٰ	Certainly (On the other hand)
مَنْ كَسَبَ	who earned
سَيِّئَةً	evil
وَ أَحَاطَتْ بِهِ	and surrounded him
خَطِيئَتُهُ	his wrongdoing

وَعَمِلُوا الصَّلِحٰتِ	and did good deeds	فَأُولَـٰئِكَ	so those are
أُولَـٰئِكَ	those are	أَصْحٰبُ	the companions of
أَصْحٰبُ الْجَنَّةِ	Companions of the Garden	اَلنَّارِ	the Fire
هُمْ فِيهَا	they (remain) in it	هُمْ فِيهَا	in it they (remain)
خٰلِدُونَ	forever	خٰلِدُونَ	forever
		وَ الَّذِينَ اٰمَنُوا	(82) And those who believed

SECTION -10-

Surah Al-Baqarah
2: 83-86

THE TEXT OF THE QUR'ĀN

بِسْمِ اللَّهِ الرَّحْمَٰنِ الرَّحِيمِ

وَإِذْ

أَخَذْنَا مِيثَاقَ بَنِي إِسْرَاءِيلَ لَا تَعْبُدُونَ إِلَّا اللَّهَ وَبِالْوَالِدَيْنِ

إِحْسَانًا وَذِي الْقُرْبَىٰ وَالْيَتَامَىٰ وَالْمَسَاكِينِ وَقُولُوا

لِلنَّاسِ حُسْنًا وَأَقِيمُوا الصَّلَاةَ وَآتُوا الزَّكَاةَ ثُمَّ

تَوَلَّيْتُمْ إِلَّا قَلِيلًا مِّنكُمْ وَأَنتُم مُّعْرِضُونَ ۞۸۳

وَإِذْ أَخَذْنَا مِيثَاقَكُمْ لَا تَسْفِكُونَ دِمَاءَكُمْ وَلَا تُخْرِجُونَ

أَنفُسَكُم مِّن دِيَارِكُمْ ثُمَّ أَقْرَرْتُمْ وَأَنتُمْ تَشْهَدُونَ ۞۸٤

ثُمَّ أَنتُمْ هَٰؤُلَاءِ تَقْتُلُونَ أَنفُسَكُمْ وَتُخْرِجُونَ فَرِيقًا

مِّنكُم مِّن دِيَارِهِمْ تَظَاهَرُونَ عَلَيْهِم بِالْإِثْمِ وَالْعُدْوَانِ

وَإِن يَأْتُوكُمْ أُسَارَىٰ تُفَادُوهُمْ وَهُوَ مُحَرَّمٌ عَلَيْكُمْ

إِخْرَاجُهُمْ أَفَتُؤْمِنُونَ بِبَعْضِ الْكِتَابِ وَتَكْفُرُونَ

بِبَعْضٍ فَمَا جَزَاءُ مَن يَفْعَلُ ذَٰلِكَ مِنكُمْ إِلَّا خِزْيٌ

فِي الْحَيَاةِ الدُّنْيَا وَيَوْمَ الْقِيَامَةِ يُرَدُّونَ إِلَىٰ أَشَدِّ الْعَذَابِ

وَمَا اللَّهُ بِغَافِلٍ عَمَّا تَعْمَلُونَ ۞۸٥ أُولَٰئِكَ الَّذِينَ اشْتَرَوُا

الْحَيَوةَ الدُّنْيَا بِالْأَخِرَةِ فَلَا يُخَفَّفُ عَنْهُمُ الْعَذَابُ وَلَاهُمْ يُنصَرُونَ ٨٦

TRANSLATIONS

Section 10: 83-86 (A. Y. Ali)

83. And remember, We took a Covenant from the Children of Israel (to this effect): worship none but Allāh; treat with kindness your parents and kindred {relatives} and orphans and those in need; speak fair to the people; be steadfast in prayer; and practice regular charity. Then did you turn back, except a few among you, and you backslide (even now).

84. And remember We took your Covenant {Mīthāq} (to this effect): shed no blood amongst you, nor turn out your own people from your homes; and this you solemnly ratified, and to this you can bear witness.

85. After this it is you, the same people, who slay among yourselves, and banish {exile, expel} a party of you from their homes; assist (their enemies) against them, in guilt and transgression; and if they come to you as captives, you ransom them, though it was not lawful for you to banish them. Then is it only a part of the Book that you believe in, and do you reject the rest? But what is the reward for those among you who behave like this but disgrace in this life? - and on the Day of Judgment, they shall be consigned to the most grievous penalty. For Allāh is not unmindful of what you do.

86. These are the people who buy the life of this world at the price of the Hereafter: their penalty shall not be lightened nor shall they be helped.

Section 10: 83-86 (M. M. Pickthall)

83. And (remember) when We made a covenant with the Children of Israel, (saying): Worship none but Allāh (only), and be good to parents and to kindred {relatives} and to orphans and the needy, and speak kindly to mankind; and establish worship and pay the poor due. Then, after that, you slid back, but a few of you, being averse.

84. And when We made with you a covenant (saying): Shed not the blood of your people nor turn (a party of) your people out of your dwellings. Then you ratified (Our covenant) and you were witnesses (thereto).

85. Yet, you it is who slay each other and drive out a party of your people from their homes, supporting one another against them by sin and transgression - and if they came to you as captives {slaves}, you would ransom them, whereas their expulsion was itself unlawful for you. Believe you in part of the Scripture and disbelieve you in part thereof? And what is the reward of those who do so but ignominy {disgrace} in the life of the world, and on the Day of Resurrection {judgement}, they will be consigned to the most grievous doom. For Allāh is not unaware of what you do.

86. Such are those who buy the life of the world at the price of the Hereafter: Their punishment will not be lightened, neither will they have support.

EXPLANATION

83: So far, the Covenant mentioned was of the kind Israelites suggested, of favors and a special relationship. However, the real Covenant is about the moral law, which is set out in 2:83. This moral law is of a universal nature. If the Israelites break it, no privileges will lighten their punishment or help them in any way (see 2:86). "Speak fair to the people" not only means outward courtesy from the leaders to

The most common among the people, but the protection of the common people from being exploited and deceived by false propaganda and wrong advertisement.

84:　　　　Verse 83 referred to the universal moral law. Verse 84 refers to its application under a special Covenant entered into with the Jews of Madinah by the newborn Muslim commonwealth under its guide and teacher, Prophet Muḥammad ﷺ. This Covenant is given in Ibn Hisham's "*Sirat ar-Rasul*", and comments on it will be found in Ameer `Ali's "Spirit of Islam", London 1922, pp. 57-61. It was entered into in the second year of the *Hijrah*, and was broken by the Jews almost immediately afterwards.

85:　　　　I understand "ransom them" here to mean "take ransom for them", though most commentators take it to mean "give ransom for them". Prophet Muḥammad ﷺ had made a pact which, if it had been faithfully observed by all parties, would have brought law and order to Madinah. But some of the unfaithful Jews never intended to observe its terms. They fought and slew each other and not only banished those who were annoying to them, but also plotted with their enemies. If, by chance, those whom they had banished came back into their hands as captives, they demanded ransom for them to return their homes, although they had had no right to banish them in the first place. If we understand by "ransom them" pay "ransom for them to release them from the hands of their enemies," it would mean that they did this pious act for show, although they were themselves the authors of their unlawful banishment. I think the former makes better sense.

86:　　　　{Working for the gains of this world by ignoring the Divine Law is a trade in which one ultimately loses. Abiding by the Law may appear hard, or at times, even harmful to self-interest, but in its ultimate end, it profoundly benefits the believer. AG}

IMPORTANT POINTS TO LEARN AND REFLECT UPON

- Allāh ﷻ has enjoined upon the Bani Isra'il, as He does upon us, to be kind to parents, relatives, the orphans and the needy and to speak to other human beings kindly.

- He has also enjoined to respect right to life and security.

- Bani Isra'il disobeyed and were punished, so would those who follow them in their defiance and disobedience.

ARABIC GLOSSARY WORDS

بِسْمِ اللهِ الرَّحْمٰنِ الرَّحِيمِ

وَ إِذْ أَخَذْنَا	(83) And when We took	وَ الْمَسٰكِين	and the poor
مِيثَاقَ	the Covenant of	وَ قُوْلُوا لِلنَّاس	and say to the people
بَنِیَ إِسْرَآءِيلَ	the Children of Israel	حُسْنًا	good
لَا تَعْبُدُونَ	you shall worship none	وَّ أَقِيمُوا الصَّلٰوةَ	and establish the *Salah*
إِلَّا اللهَ	but Allah	وَ اٰتُوا الزَّكٰوةَ	and pay the *zakah*
وَبِالْوَالِدَيْنِ	and with your parents	ثُمَّ تَوَلَّيْتُمْ	then you turned away
إِحْسَانًا	do good	إِلَّا قَلِيلًا	except a few
وَّ ذِى الْقُرْبٰى	and to kindred	مِّنْكُمْ	among you
وَ الْيَتٰمٰى	and the orphans	وَ أَنْتُمْ مُّعْرِضُونَ	and you are (still) backsliding

وَ إِذْ (84)	And remember when
أَخَذْنَا	We took
مِيثَاقَكُمْ	your covenant
لَا تَسْفِكُونَ	you shall not shed
دِمَاءَكُمْ	your blood,
	(kill your own people)
وَ لَا تُخْرِجُونَ	nor you shall expel
أَنْفُسَكُمْ	your persons
مِنْ دِيَارِكُمْ	from your homes
ثُمَّ	then
أَقْرَرْتُمْ	you ratified (it)
وَ أَنْتُمْ تَشْهَدُونَ	and you bear witness
ثُمَّ أَنْتُمْ هَؤُلَاءِ (85)	Then it is you who
تَقْتُلُونَ أَنْفُسَكُمْ	kill your men (lit. yourselves)
وَ تُخْرِجُونَ	and you expel
فَرِيقًا	a group (a party)
مِنْكُمْ	of you
مِنْ دِيَارِهِمْ	from their homes
تَظَاهَرُونَ عَلَيْهِمْ	supporting one another
	against them
بِالْإِثْمِ	in sin
وَ الْعُدْوَانِ	and aggnession
وَ إِنْ يَأْتُوكُمْ	and if they come to you
أُسَارَى	(as) prisoners
تُفَادُوهُمْ	you ransom them
وَ هُوَ	and it was (already)
مُحَرَّمٌ عَلَيْكُمْ	unlawful upon (for) you

إِخْرَاجُهُمْ	to expel them
أَفَتُؤْمِنُونَ	do you believe?
بِبَعْضِ الْكِتَابِ	in one part of the Book
وَتَكْفُرُونَ	and you deny
بِبَعْضٍ	the other part of it (lit. some)
فَمَا	then what (could be)
جَزَاءُ	the reward
مَنْ يَفْعَلُ	(of one) who does
ذَلِكَ	that
مِنْكُمْ	among you
إِلَّا الْأَخْزَى	except disgrace (humiliation)
فِى الْحَيَوةِ الدُّنْيَا	in the life of this world
وَيَوْمَ الْقِيَمَةِ	and (on) the Day of Resurrection
يُرَدُّونَ	they will be driven
إِلَى	to
أَشَدِّ الْعَذَابِ	the harshest torment
وَمَا اللهُ	and Allah is not
بِغَافِلٍ	unaware
عَمَّا تَعْمَلُونَ	of what you do
أُولَئِكَ الَّذِينَ (86)	Those are the ones who
اشْتَرَوُا	bought
الْحَيَوةَ الدُّنْيَا	the life of this world
بِالْآخِرَةِ	with the Hereafter
فَلَا يُخَفَّفُ	so shall not be lightened
عَنْهُمُ الْعَذَابُ	for them the punishment
وَ لَا هُمْ يُنْصَرُونَ	nor they shall be helped

SECTION -11-

Sūrah Al-Baqarah
2: 87-96

THE TEXT OF THE QUR'ĀN

بِسْمِ اللَّهِ الرَّحْمَٰنِ الرَّحِيمِ

وَلَقَدْ ءَاتَيْنَا مُوسَى الْكِتَٰبَ وَقَفَّيْنَا مِنۢ

بَعْدِهِۦ بِالرُّسُلِ وَءَاتَيْنَا عِيسَى ابْنَ مَرْيَمَ الْبَيِّنَٰتِ وَأَيَّدْنَٰهُ

بِرُوحِ الْقُدُسِ أَفَكُلَّمَا جَآءَكُمْ رَسُولٌۢ بِمَا لَا تَهْوَىٰ أَنفُسُكُمُ

اسْتَكْبَرْتُمْ فَفَرِيقًا كَذَّبْتُمْ وَفَرِيقًا تَقْتُلُونَ ۝ وَقَالُوا

قُلُوبُنَا غُلْفٌۢ بَل لَّعَنَهُمُ اللَّهُ بِكُفْرِهِمْ فَقَلِيلًا مَّا يُؤْمِنُونَ ۝

وَلَمَّا جَآءَهُمْ كِتَٰبٌ مِّنْ عِندِ اللَّهِ مُصَدِّقٌ لِّمَا مَعَهُمْ وَكَانُوا

مِن قَبْلُ يَسْتَفْتِحُونَ عَلَى الَّذِينَ كَفَرُوا فَلَمَّا جَآءَهُم

مَّا عَرَفُوا كَفَرُوا بِهِۦ فَلَعْنَةُ اللَّهِ عَلَى الْكَٰفِرِينَ ۝

بِئْسَمَا اشْتَرَوْا بِهِۦٓ أَنفُسَهُمْ أَن يَكْفُرُوا بِمَآ أَنزَلَ

اللَّهُ بَغْيًا أَن يُنَزِّلَ اللَّهُ مِن فَضْلِهِۦ عَلَىٰ مَن يَشَآءُ مِنْ عِبَادِهِۦ

فَبَآءُو بِغَضَبٍ عَلَىٰ غَضَبٍ وَلِلْكَٰفِرِينَ عَذَابٌ مُّهِينٌ

۝ وَإِذَا قِيلَ لَهُمْ ءَامِنُوا بِمَآ أَنزَلَ اللَّهُ قَالُوا نُؤْمِنُ بِمَآ

أُنزِلَ عَلَيْنَا وَيَكْفُرُونَ بِمَا وَرَآءَهُۥ وَهُوَ الْحَقُّ مُصَدِّقًا

لِّمَا مَعَهُمْ قُلْ فَلِمَ تَقْتُلُونَ أَنۢبِيَآءَ اللَّهِ مِن قَبْلُ إِن كُنتُم

مُّؤْمِنِينَ ﴿٩١﴾ وَلَقَدْ جَآءَكُم مُّوسَىٰ بِٱلْبَيِّنَٰتِ

ثُمَّ ٱتَّخَذْتُمُ ٱلْعِجْلَ مِنۢ بَعْدِهِۦ وَأَنتُمْ ظَٰلِمُونَ ﴿٩٢﴾

وَإِذْ أَخَذْنَا مِيثَٰقَكُمْ وَرَفَعْنَا فَوْقَكُمُ ٱلطُّورَ خُذُوا۟

مَآ ءَاتَيْنَٰكُم بِقُوَّةٍ وَٱسْمَعُوا۟ قَالُوا۟ سَمِعْنَا وَعَصَيْنَا

وَأُشْرِبُوا۟ فِى قُلُوبِهِمُ ٱلْعِجْلَ بِكُفْرِهِمْ قُلْ

بِئْسَمَا يَأْمُرُكُم بِهِۦٓ إِيمَٰنُكُمْ إِن كُنتُم مُّؤْمِنِينَ ﴿٩٣﴾

قُلْ إِن كَانَتْ لَكُمُ ٱلدَّارُ ٱلْءَاخِرَةُ عِندَ ٱللَّهِ خَالِصَةً مِّن

دُونِ ٱلنَّاسِ فَتَمَنَّوُا۟ ٱلْمَوْتَ إِن كُنتُمْ صَٰدِقِينَ ﴿٩٤﴾

وَلَن يَتَمَنَّوْهُ أَبَدًۢا بِمَا قَدَّمَتْ أَيْدِيهِمْ وَٱللَّهُ عَلِيمٌۢ بِٱلظَّٰلِمِينَ

﴿٩٥﴾ وَلَتَجِدَنَّهُمْ أَحْرَصَ ٱلنَّاسِ عَلَىٰ حَيَوٰةٍ وَمِنَ ٱلَّذِينَ

أَشْرَكُوا۟ يَوَدُّ أَحَدُهُمْ لَوْ يُعَمَّرُ أَلْفَ سَنَةٍ وَمَا هُوَ بِمُزَحْزِحِهِۦ

مِنَ ٱلْعَذَابِ أَن يُعَمَّرَ وَٱللَّهُ بَصِيرٌۢ بِمَا يَعْمَلُونَ ﴿٩٦﴾

TRANSLATIONS

Section 11: 87-96 (A. Y. Ali)

87. We gave Moses the Book and followed him up with a succession of Messengers; We gave Jesus, the son of Mary, clear (Signs) and strengthened him with the Holy Spirit {Angel} Is it that whenever there comes

Section 11: 87-96 (M. M. Pickthall)

87. And verily, We gave unto Moses the Scripture and We caused a train of messengers to follow after him, and We gave unto Jesus, son of Mary, clear proofs (of Allāh's sovereignty), and We supported him with the

to you a Messenger with what you yourselves desire not, you are puffed up with pride? - Some you called imposters {trickery} and others you slay!

88. They say, "Our hearts are the wrappings (which preserve Allah's word: we need no more)." Surely, Allāh's curse is on them for their blasphemy: little is it they believe.

89. And when there comes to them a Book from Allāh, confirming what is with them - although from of old they had prayed for victory against those without Faith {*Kafarū*} when there comes to them that which they (should) have recognized. They refuse to believe in it but the curse of Allāh is on those without Faith.

90. Miserable is the price for which they have sold their souls, in that they deny (the revelation) which Allāh has sent down, in insolent {rude, disrespectful} envy that Allāh of His Grace should send it to any of His servants He pleases: thus have they drawn on themselves wrath upon wrath, and humiliating is the punishment of those who reject Faith.

91. When it is said to them, "believe in what Allāh has sent down," they say, "We believe in what was sent down to us;" yet they reject all besides, even if it be truth confirming what is with them. Say: "Why then have you slain the prophets of Allāh in times gone by, if you did indeed believe?"

92. There came to you Moses with clear (Signs); yet you worshipped the Calf (even) after that, and you did behave wrongfully.

93. And remember We took your Covenant and We raised above you (the towering height) of Mount (Sinai): (saying): "Hold firmly to what We have given you and hearken {hear} (to the Law)": they said: "We hear, and we disobey": and they had to drink into their hearts (of the taint) of the calf because of their faithlessness. Say: "Vile {evil} indeed are the behests of your faith, if you have any

holy Spirit. Is it ever so, that, when there comes unto you a messenger (from Allāh) with that which you yourselves desire not, you grow arrogant, and some you disbelieve and some you slay?

88. And they say: Our hearts are hardened. Surely, but Allāh has cursed them for their unbelief. Little is that which they believe.

89. And when there comes unto them a Scripture from Allāh, confirming that in their possession - though before that they were asking for a signal triumph over those who disbelieved - and when there comes unto them that which they know (to be the Truth) they disbelieve therein. The curse of Allāh is on disbelievers.

90. Evil is that for which they sell their souls: that they should disbelieve in that which Allāh has revealed, grudging that Allāh should reveal of His bounty {generosity} unto whom He will of His bondmen. They have incurred anger upon anger. For disbelievers is a shameful doom.

91. And when it is said unto them: Believe in that which Allāh has revealed, they say: We believe in that which was revealed unto us. And they disbelieve in that which comes after it, though it is the truth confirming that which they possess. Say (unto them, O Muḥammad): Why then slew you the Prophets of Allāh aforetime, if you are (indeed) believers?

92. And Moses came unto you with clear proofs (of Allah's sovereignty), yet, while he was away, you chose the calf (for worship) and you were wrongdoers.

93. And when We made with you a covenant and caused the Mount to tower above you, (saying): Hold fast by that which We have given you, and hear (Our Word), they said: We hear and we rebel. And (worship of) the calf was made to sink into their hearts because of their rejection (of the Covenant). Say (unto them): Evil is that which your belief enjoins on you, if you are believers.

faith!"

94. Say: "If the last Home, with Allāh {the Paradise} be for you specially, and not for anyone else, then seek you for death, if you are sincere."

95. But they will never seek for death, on account of the (sins) which their hands have sent on before them. And Allāh is well-acquainted with the wrongdoers.

96. You will indeed find them, of all people, most greedy of life - even more than the idolaters: each one of them wishes he could be given a life of a thousand years: but the grant of such life will not save him from (due) punishment. For Allāh sees well {*Baṣir*} all that they do.

94. Say (unto them): If the abode {dwelling} of the Hereafter {the Paradise} in the providence {judgement} of Allāh is indeed for you alone and not for others of mankind (as you pretend), then seek for death (for you must seek for death) if you are truthful.

95. But they will never seek for it, because of that which their own hands have sent before them. Allāh is Aware {*Al-'Alīm*} of evil-doers.

96. And you will find them greediest of mankind for life and (greedier) than the idolaters. (Each) one of them would like to be allowed to live a thousand years. And to live (a thousand years) would by no means remove him from the doom. Allāh is Seer {Watchful} of what they do.

EXPLANATION

87: As to the birth of Jesus, see 19:16-34. Why is he called the "Son of Mary"? What are his "clear signs"? What is the "holy spirit" by which he was strengthened? Jesus is no more than a man. It is against reason and revelation to call him a god or a son of a god. He is called the son of Mary to emphasize this fact. His miraculous birth does not raise him to divinity but testifies to Allāh's power. Allāh has created Ādam and Eve without a father and a mother (See also, 3:62), and Christians don't believe them to be god. {Jesus, like other Prophets was supported by the holy spirit, angel Gabriel (Jibril). AG}. Reviewing the long course of Jewish history, we now come to the time of Jesus. The Jews often mistreated, lied to and disobeyed God's messengers, and they even tried to slay Jesus. 2:87-121 refers to the People of the Book generally, Jews and Christians; they should have welcomed Prophet Muḥammad's teachings, and yet, the majority of them took up an attitude of arrogant rejection.

88: The Jews, in their arrogance, claimed that all wisdom and all knowledge of God was enclosed in their hearts. But there are more things in heaven and earth than were dreamed of in their philosophy. Ibn Kathir comments that this verse refers to the Jewish claim that a covering had been placed over their hearts, preventing them from grasping the message of Prophet Muḥammad. See also 4:155. AG.}

89: The root *kafara* has many shades of meaning: (1) to deny God's goodness, to be ungrateful, (2) to reject Faith, deny His revelation, (3) to blaspheme, to ascribe some limitation or attribute to God which is derogatory to His nature. In a translation, one shade or another must be put forward according to the context, but all are implied. The Jews, who received earlier revelations, and who claimed to be superior to the people without Faith - the gentiles - should have been the first to recognize the Truth of the new revelation. The mission of the Prophet Muḥammad was similar in form and language to what they had already received. But they had more arrogance than faith. Again, the lesson applies to a much wider circle than the Jews. We are all apt, in our pride, to reject an appeal from our brother without considering one from an outsider. If we have a glimmer of the truth, we often make ourselves imperious to further truth.

90: The lesson is wider than Jewish rejection of the Truth. Is that rejection unknown in our own times, and among other races? Yet, how can a race or a people put boundaries on God's choices?

91: Even the race argument is often a flimsy and hollow pretext. Did not the Jews reject prophets of their own race who told them unpleasant truths? And do not other nations do likewise?

92-93: Here, they are reminded of the same solemn Covenant (as in 2:63). They said in words: "All that the Lord has spoken, we will do" But they said in their hearts: "We shall disobey". What they should have said was: "We hear, and we obey". This is the attitude of the true people of Faith (see 2:285). After the Commandments and the Law had been given at Mount Sinai, and the people had solemnly given their Covenant. Yet, when Moses went up to the Mount, the people made the golden calf in his absence. When Moses returned, his anger waxed hot. "He took the calf, which they had made, burned it in the fire, ground it to powder, strewed it upon the water, and made the children of Israel drink of it." (Exod. 32:20).

94:     {A true Believer does not fear death. His true faith and good deeds make Him desire death in the path of God and a longing to meet Him. AG}.

95:     The phrase "What their hands have sent on before them" frequently occurs in the Qur'ān. Here, and in many places, it refers to sins. In such passages as *An-Naba'* 78:40, or *Luqmān* 31:14, it is implied that both good and bad deeds go before us to the judgement seat of God before we ourselves do. In 2:110, it is the good that goes before us. Our deeds are personified. They are witnesses for or against us, and they always go before us.

96:     {For a faithful person, this world is like a prison, but for the unfaithful, it is a life of freedom. The Jews loved most the life of this world and were scared of the idea of death. However, death and judgment are certainties that no one can escape. AG}

IMPORTANT POINTS TO LEARN AND REFLECT UPON

- Whenever a prophet or a revelation of Allāh ﷻ came to Bani Isrā'il, they denied and disobeyed them.

- Those who are engrossed in worldly pleasures are most desirous of this life; but the death and judgment is a certainty.

- Those who believe and do good deeds are most desirous to meet Allāh ﷻ.

ARABIC GLOSSARY WORDS

بِسْمِ اللهِ الرَّحْمٰنِ الرَّحِيمِ

وَ لَقَدْ اَتَيْنَا	(87) And indeed We gave	جَآءَكُمْ رَسُوْلٌ	came to you a messenger
مُوسَى الْكِتٰبَ	Moses the Book	بِمَا لاَ تَهْوٰى	with what do not fancy
وَقَفَّيْنَا	and we caused a train of	اَنْفُسُكُمْ	yourselves
مِنْ بَعْدِه	to follow after him	اِسْتَكْبَرْتُمْ	you were arrogant (to accept it)
بِالرُّسُلِ	messengers	فَفَرِيقًا	so a party (a group of prophets)
وَ اٰتَيْنَا عِيسَى	and We gave Jesus	كَذَّبْتُمْ	you repudiated
ابْنَ مَرْيَمَ	son of Mary	وَفَرِيقًا	and a group of prophets
الْبَيِّنٰتِ	the clear (signs)	تَقْتُلُوْنَ	you kill
وَ أَيَّدْنٰهُ	and supported him	وَ قَالُوْا	(88) And they said
بِرُوْحِ الْقُدُسِ	with the Holy Spirit	قُلُوْبُنَا غُلْفٌ	our hearts are covered
أَفَكُلَّمَا	is it the case that whenever	بَلْ لَعَنَهُمُ اللهُ	No, Allah cursed them

فَبَآءُوْ بِغَضَبٍ	Thus they incurred	بِكُفْرِهِمْ	due to their disbelief
	(upon themselves) Wrath	فَقَلِيْلًا	so very seldom
عَلَى غَضَبٍ	after Wrath	مَّا يُؤْمِنُوْنَ	they believe
وَ لِلْكَفِرِيْنَ	and for the disbelievers	وَ لَمَّا جَآءَهُمْ	(89) And when came to them
عَذَابٌ مُّهِيْنٌ	disgraceful punishment	كِتَبٌ	a Book
(91)وَ إِذَا قِيْلَ لَهُمْ	And when it is said to them	مِنْ عِنْدِ اللهِ	from Allah
امِنُوْا بِمَآ	believe in what	مُصَدِّقٌ	testifying to
أَنْزَلَ اللهُ	Allah sent down	لِمَا مَعَهُمْ	what is with them
قَالُوْا نُؤْمِنُ	they said we believe	وَكَانُوْا	and they were
بِمَآ أُنْزِلَ	in what is sent down	مِنْ قَبْلُ	before this
عَلَيْنَا	on us	يَسْتَفْتِحُوْنَ	praying for victory
وَيَكْفُرُوْنَ	and they disbelieve	عَلَى الَّذِيْنَ كَفَرُوْا	over those who disbelieved
بِمَا وَرَآءَهُ	in other than it	فَلَمَّا جَآءَهُمْ	so when came to them
وَهُوَ الْحَقُّ	even though it is the truth	مَّا عَرَفُوْا	what they recognized
مُصَدِّقًا	confirming	كَفَرُوْا بِهِ	they disbelieved
لِمَا مَعَهُمْ	what is with them	فَلَعْنَةُ اللهِ	so Allah's curse
قُلْ	say	عَلَى الْكَفِرِيْنَ	on the disbelievers
فَلِمَ تَقْتُلُوْنَ	then why (were) you killing	بِئْسَمَا (90)	What a wretched (thing) it was
أَنْبِيَآءَ اللهِ	Prophets of Allah	اشْتَرَوْا بِهِ	with which they bought
مِنْ قَبْلُ	in the past	أَنْفُسَهُمْ	their own selves
إِنْ كُنْتُمْ مُؤْمِنِيْنَ	if you are believers	أَنْ يَّكْفُرُوْا بِمَا	that they disbelieved in
وَ لَقَدْ (92)	And indeed	أَنْزَلَ اللهُ	what Allah sent down
جَآءَكُمْ مُوْسَى	Moses came to you	بَغْيًا	begrudging
بِالْبَيِّنَتِ	with clear (signs)	أَنْ يُنَزِّلَ اللهُ	that Allah should send
ثُمَّ	then	مِنْ	out of (from)
اتَّخَذْتُمُ	you took (for worship)	فَضْلِهِ	His Favor
الْعِجْلَ	the calf	عَلَى مَنْ يَّشَآءُ	on whom He wills
مِنْ بَعْدِهِ	after him (after he left)	مِنْ عِبَادِهِ	among His servants,

وَ أَنْتُمْ ظٰلِمُونَ	and you were unjust
وَ إِذْ أَخَذْنَا	(93) And when We took
مِيثَاقَكُمْ	your covenant
وَرَفَعْنَا	and we raised
فَوْقَكُمْ	above you
الطُّورَ	the Mount (Sinai)
خُذُوا	hold to
مَا آتَيْنٰكُمْ	what We gave you
بِقُوَّةٍ وَّ اسْمَعُوا	with strength and listen
قَالُوا سَمِعْنَا	they said we listened
وَعَصَيْنَا	and we disobeyed
وَ أُشْرِبُوا	and are imbued with
فِى قُلُوبِهِمُ	their hearts
الْعِجْلَ	(the love of) the calf
بِكُفْرِهِمْ	due to their disbelief
قُلْ بِئْسَمَا	say evil is that
يَأْمُرُكُمْ بِهِ	orders you to do it
إِيمَانُكُمْ	your belief
إِنْ كُنْتُمْ مُؤْمِنِينَ	if you are believers
قُلْ (94)	Say
إِنْ كَانَتْ	if (it) was
لَكُمُ	for you
الدَّارُ الْآخِرَةُ	the House of the Hereafter
عِنْدَ الله	with Allah
خَالِصَةً	purely (exclusively for you)
مِنْ دُونِ	excluding the (rest of)

النَّاسِ	humankind
فَتَمَنَّوُا الْمَوْتَ	then desire for death
إِنْ كُنْتُمْ	if you are
صَادِقِينَ	truthful
وَ لَنْ يَتَمَنَّوْهُ	(95) And they will
	never desire for it
أَبَدًا	ever
بِمَا قَدَّمَتْ	because of what advanced
أَيْدِيهِمْ	their hands
وَ اللهُ عَلِيمٌ	and Allah knows
بِالظّٰلِمِينَ	the unjust people
وَ(96)And you will definitely find them	وَلَتَجِدَنَّهُمْ
أَحْرَصَ	most greedy
النَّاسِ	(out of) all people
عَلَى حَيٰوةٍ	for life
وَمِنَ الَّذِينَ	and than those
أَشْرَكُوا	who are pagans
يَوَدُّ أَحَدُهُمْ	wishes one of them
لَوْ يُعَمَّرُ	if he could live
أَلْفَ سَنَةٍ	one thousand years
وَمَا هُوَ	and (it will) not
بِمُزَحْزِحِهِ	move him away
مِنَ الْعَذَابِ	from the Punishment
أَنْ يُّعَمَّرَ	that he lives long
وَ اللهُ بَصِيرٌ	and Allah is Seer
بِمَا يَعْمَلُونَ	(of) what they do

SECTION -12-

Surah Al-Baqarah
2: 97-103

THE TEXT OF THE QUR'ĀN

بِسْمِ اللهِ الرَّحْمٰنِ الرَّحِيمِ

قُلْ

مَن كَانَ عَدُوًّا لِّجِبْرِيلَ فَإِنَّهُ نَزَّلَهُ عَلَىٰ قَلْبِكَ بِإِذْنِ اللهِ

مُصَدِّقًا لِّمَا بَيْنَ يَدَيْهِ وَهُدًى وَبُشْرَىٰ لِلْمُؤْمِنِينَ

۹۷ مَن كَانَ عَدُوًّا لِّلَّهِ وَمَلَٰئِكَتِهِ وَرُسُلِهِ وَجِبْرِيلَ

وَمِيكَىٰلَ فَإِنَّ اللهَ عَدُوٌّ لِّلْكَٰفِرِينَ ۹۸ وَلَقَدْ أَنزَلْنَا

إِلَيْكَ ءَايَٰتٍ بَيِّنَٰتٍ وَمَا يَكْفُرُ بِهَا إِلَّا ٱلْفَٰسِقُونَ ۹۹

أَوَكُلَّمَا عَٰهَدُوا۟ عَهْدًا نَّبَذَهُ فَرِيقٌ مِّنْهُم بَلْ أَكْثَرُهُمْ

لَا يُؤْمِنُونَ ۱۰۰ وَلَمَّا جَآءَهُمْ رَسُولٌ مِّنْ عِندِ اللهِ

مُصَدِّقٌ لِّمَا مَعَهُمْ نَبَذَ فَرِيقٌ مِّنَ ٱلَّذِينَ أُوتُوا۟ ٱلْكِتَٰبَ

كِتَٰبَ اللهِ وَرَآءَ ظُهُورِهِمْ كَأَنَّهُمْ لَا يَعْلَمُونَ ۱۰۱

وَٱتَّبَعُوا۟ مَا تَتْلُوا۟ ٱلشَّيَٰطِينُ عَلَىٰ مُلْكِ سُلَيْمَٰنَ وَمَا كَفَرَ

سُلَيْمَٰنُ وَلَٰكِنَّ ٱلشَّيَٰطِينَ كَفَرُوا۟ يُعَلِّمُونَ ٱلنَّاسَ

ٱلسِّحْرَ وَمَآ أُنزِلَ عَلَى ٱلْمَلَكَيْنِ بِبَابِلَ هَٰرُوتَ وَمَٰرُوتَ

وَمَا يُعَلِّمَانِ مِنْ أَحَدٍ حَتَّىٰ يَقُولَا إِنَّمَا نَحْنُ فِتْنَةٌ فَلَا تَكْفُرْ

فَيَتَعَلَّمُونَ مِنْهُمَا مَا يُفَرِّقُونَ بِهِ بَيْنَ الْمَرْءِ وَزَوْجِهِ

وَمَا هُم بِضَارِّينَ بِهِ مِنْ أَحَدٍ إِلَّا بِإِذْنِ اللَّهِ وَيَتَعَلَّمُونَ

مَا يَضُرُّهُمْ وَلَا يَنفَعُهُمْ وَلَقَدْ عَلِمُوا لَمَنِ اشْتَرَاهُ

مَا لَهُ فِي الْآخِرَةِ مِنْ خَلَاقٍ وَلَبِئْسَ مَا شَرَوْا بِهِ

أَنفُسَهُمْ لَوْ كَانُوا يَعْلَمُونَ ۝١٠٢ وَلَوْ أَنَّهُمْ آمَنُوا

وَاتَّقَوْا لَمَثُوبَةٌ مِّنْ عِندِ اللَّهِ خَيْرٌ لَّوْ كَانُوا يَعْلَمُونَ

TRANSLATIONS

Section 12: 97-103 (A. Y. Ali)

97. Say: Whoever is an enemy to Gabriel {Jibril} - for he brings down the (revelation) to your heart by Allāh's will, a confirmation of what went before, and guidance and glad tidings for those who believe -

98. Whoever is an enemy to Allāh and His angels and prophets, {Messengers} to Gabriel and Michael {Mikā'il}- Lo! Allāh is an enemy to those who reject Faith.

99. We have sent down to you manifest Signs (`Ayāt); and none reject them but those who are perverse {corrupted}

100. Is it not (the case) that every time they make a Covenant, some party among them throw it aside? - Surely, most of them are faithless.

101. And when there came to them a Messenger from Allāh, confirming what was with them, a party of the People of the Book threw away the Book of Allāh behind their backs. As if (it had been something) they did not

Section 12: 97-103 (M. M. Pickthall)

97. Say (O Muḥammad to mankind): Who is an enemy to Gabriel {Jibril}! For he it is who has revealed (this Scripture) to your heart by Allāh's leave {will}, confirming that which was (revealed) before it, and a guidance and glad tidings to believers;

98. Who is an enemy to Allāh, and His angels and His messengers, and Gabriel and Michael {Mikā'il}! Then, lo! Allāh (Himself) is an enemy to the disbelievers.

99. Verily, We have revealed unto you clear Tokens {Signs}, and only miscreants {corrupt ones} will disbelieve in them.

100. Is it ever so that when you make a covenant a party of you set it aside? The truth is, most of them believe not.

101. And when there comes unto them a Messenger from Allāh, confirming that which they possess, a party of those who have received the Scripture fling the Scripture of Allāh behind their backs as if they knew not,

know!

102. They followed what the evil ones gave out (falsely) against the power of Solomon: the blasphemers were, not Solomon, but the evil ones, teaching men magic, and such things as came down at Babylon to the angels Hārūt and Mārūt. But neither of these taught anyone (such things) without saying: "We are only for trial; so do not blaspheme {disbelieve}" They learned from them the means to sow discord between man and wife. But they could not thus harm anyone except by Allāh's permission. And they learned what harmed them, not what profited them. And they knew that the buyers of (magic) would have no share in the happiness of the Hereafter. And vile was the price for which they did sell their souls, if they but knew!

103. If they had kept their faith and guarded themselves from evil, far better had been the reward from their Lord, if they but knew!

102. And follow that which the devils falsely related against the kingdom of Solomon. Solomon disbelieved not; but the devils disbelieved, teaching mankind magic and that which was revealed to the two angels in Babel, Hārūt and Mārūt. Nor did they (the two angels) teach it to anyone till they had said: We are only a temptation. Therefore, disbelieve not (in the guidance of Allāh). And from these two (angels) people learn that by which they cause division between man and wife; but they injure thereby no one but by Allāh's leave. And they learn that which harms them and profits them not. And surely they do know that he who traffics therein will have no (happy) portion in the Hereafter; and surely evil is the price for which they sell their souls, if they but knew.

103. And if they had believed and kept from evil, a recompense {reward} from Allāh would be better, if they only knew.

EXPLANATION

97-98: During the time of Prophet Muḥammad ﷺ a party of the Jews ridiculed the Muslim belief that Gabriel brought down revelations to Prophet Muḥammad ﷺ. Michael was called in their books "the great prince who stands for the children of your people" (Daniel 12:1). However, the vision of Gabriel inspired fear and hostility (Daniel, 8:16-17). Angel Gabriel was only a messenger of God, and those who are hostile to him earn the hostility of God.

99: The message of Islām and the exemplary life of Prophet Muḥammad ﷺ were clear Signs which everyone could understand, except those who were obstinate. Moreover, the verses of the Qur'ān were reasonable and clear.

100: {The history of the Israelites and strong criticism of the Prophets testifies to the fact of their first accepting the Divine Covenants, but later rejecting them for a small gain or demand of sacrifice. AG}

101: The argument is that if the Jews had looked into their own Books honestly and sincerely, they would have found proofs in them to show that the new Message was true and from God. Instead, they ignored them or twisted them to suit to their own fancies.

102: The People of the Book, instead of following the Revelations, ran after all sorts of occult knowledge, most of which was false and evil. Many tales of occult power attributed the power of Prophet Solomon ﷺ to magic. Solomon ﷺ was God's chosen prophet and did not deal in arts of evil. This verse has been interpreted variously. Who were Hārūt and Mārūt? What did they teach? Why did they teach it? The view which I find convincing that of the *Tafsīr Haqqānī* following Baidāwi and the *Tafsīr Kabīr*. The word "angels" as applied to Hārūt and Mārūt is figurative. It means "good men, of knowledge, science (or wisdom) and power." The knowledge that the evil ones gained from Hārūt and Mārūt, they put to the use of evil, creating discord between the sexes. But of course their power was limited to the extent to which God permitted the evil to work, for His grace protected all who sought His guidance and repented and returned to Him.

The Evil Ones used what they learned from Hārūt and Mārūt (see last note) for evil. Combined with fraud and deception, the evil appeared as charms which caused discord between the couples. Their power was limited to the extent to which God permitted the evil to work; His Mercy protected all who sought His guidance. Apart from the harm that these false pretenders did to others, the chief harm which they did was to their own souls; not only to their own souls, but to the souls of all who followed them.

103: {To keep faith with God always works to our advantage, even though its benefits may not be obvious to us immediately. AG. The temptation of immediate gain often leads people to follow the wrong course. They forget the everlasting benefits that come from guarding themselves against evil and waiting for the true reward from Allāh ﷻ. AG}.

IMPORTANT POINTS TO LEARN AND REFLECT UPON

- Allāh ﷻ revealed the Qur'ān on the heart of the Prophet ﷺ ; it confirms the Truth of the past revelations and gives guidance and good news for the believers.

- To have hostility for the angels of Allāh ﷻ is to show hostility toward Allāh's ﷻ Plans.

- The messengers do not teach magic, they deliver Allāh's ﷺ message of guidance for the benefit of humanity.

ARABIC GLOSSARY WORDS

بِسْمِ اللهِ الرَّحْمٰنِ الرَّحِيمِ

قُلْ مَنْ كَانَ	(97)Say whosoever is	عَدُوًّا لِّلّٰهِ	an enemy to Allah
عَدُوًّا لِّجِبْرِيلَ	an enemy to Gabriel	وَ مَلٰئِكَتِهِ	and His angels
فَإِنَّهُ	so, in fact, he	وَرُسُلِهِ	and His messengers
نَزَّلَهُ	brought it down	وَجِبْرِيلَ وَمِيكٰلَ	and Gabriel and Michael
عَلٰى قَلْبِكَ	on your heart	فَإِنَّ اللّٰهَ	so indeed Allah is
بِإِذْنِ	by command	عَدُوٌّ	enemy
اللهِ	(of) Allah	لِّلْكٰفِرِينَ	to (these) disbelievers
مُصَدِّقًا	confirming the truth	(99) وَ لَقَدْ	And surely
لِّمَا	of what	أَنْزَلْنَآ	We have sent down
بَيْنَ يَدَيْهِ	(is) before it	إِلَيْكَ	to you
وَهُدًى وَّ بُشْرٰى	and guidance and good news	ايٰتٍ بَيِّنٰتٍ	clear signs
		وَّ مَا يَكْفُرُ	and none disbelieves
لِلْمُؤْمِنِينَ	to the believers	بِهَآ	in it
(98) مَنْ كَانَ	Whosoever is	إِلَّا الْفٰسِقُونَ	except the vicious people

(100) أَوَ كُلَّمَا	Is it the case that whenever
عَهَدُوا عَهْدًا	they made a covenant
نَّبَذَهُ فَرِيقٌ	disregarded it a party
مِنْهُمْ	among them
بَلْ أَكْثَرُهُمْ	rather most of them
لَا يُؤْمِنُونَ	do not believe
(101) وَ لَمَّا جَاءَهُمْ	And when came to them
رَسُولٌ	a messenger
مِنْ عِنْدِ الله	(especially) from Allah
مُصَدِّقٌ لِّمَا	confirming (to) what is
مَعَهُمْ	with them
نَبَذَ فَرِيقٌ مِنَ	threw (disregarded) a group
مِنَ الَّذِينَ أُوتُوا	among those who were given
الْكِتَبَ	the Book
كِتَبَ الله	the Book of Allah
وَرَاءَ ظُهُورِهِمْ	(throwing it) behind their backs
كَأَنَّهُمْ لَا يَعْلَمُونَ	as if they do not know
(102) وَ اتَّبَعُوا	And they followed
مَا تَتْلُوا	what (used to) recite
الشَّيَطِينُ	the satans
عَلَى مُلْكِ سُلَيْمَنَ	over (during) Solomon's reign
وَمَا كَفَرَ سُلَيْمَنُ	and Solomon did not disbelieve
وَ لَكِنَّ الشَّيَطِينَ	but the satans
كَفَرُوا	disbelieved
يُعَلِّمُونَ النَّاسَ	they (used to) teach people
السِّحْرَ	the magic
وَ مَا أُنْزِلَ	and what was sent (down)
عَلَى الْمَلَكَيْنِ	on the two angels
بِبَابِلَ	in Babylon
هَارُوتَ وَمَارُوتَ	Harut and Marut
وَ مَا يُعَلِّمَنِ	and they (both) did not teach
مِنْ أَحَدٍ	anyone
حَتَّى يَقُولَا	until they said
إِنَّمَا نَحْنُ فِتْنَةٌ	we are only a trial
فَلَا تَكْفُرْ	so do not disbelieve
فَيَتَعَلَّمُونَ	so they used to learn
مِنْهُمَا	from those two
مَا يُفَرِّقُونَ	they caused division
بِهِ	that by
بَيْنَ الْمَرْءِ	between the man
وَزَوْجِهِ	and his wife
وَمَا هُمْ	and they did not
بِضَارِّينَ بِهِ	harm with it
مِنْ أَحَدٍ إِلَّا	anyone except
بِإِذْنِ الله	with the permission of Allah
وَيَتَعَلَّمُونَ	and they used to learn
مَا يَضُرُّهُمْ	what would harm them
وَ لَا يَنْفَعُهُمْ	and would not profit them
وَ لَقَدْ عَلِمُوا	and indeed they knew
لَمَنِ اشْتَرَهُ	that whoever buys it
مَالَهُ	there is nothing for him
فِي الْآخِرَةِ	in the Hereafter
مِنْ خَلَاقٍ	from a share (of happiness)
وَ لَبِئْسَ	and surely what an evil thing
مَا شَرَوْا بِهِ	with which they put at bargain
أَنْفُسَهُمْ	their (own)selves

لَوْ كَانُوا يَعْلَمُونَ	if they had known it	مِنْ عِنْدِاللهِ	from Allah
وَلَوْ أَنَّهُمْ اٰمَنُوا	(103) And had they believed	خَيْرٌ	(was) better
وَاتَّقَوْا	developed *taqwa*	لَوْ كَانُوا يَعْلَمُونَ	if they had known it
لَمَثُوبَةٌ	surely reward		

SECTION -13-

Sūrah Al-Baqarah
2: 104-112

THE TEXT OF THE QUR'ĀN

بِسْمِ اللَّهِ الرَّحْمَٰنِ الرَّحِيمِ

يَٰٓأَيُّهَا ٱلَّذِينَ ءَامَنُوا۟ لَا تَقُولُوا۟ رَٰعِنَا وَقُولُوا۟ ٱنظُرْنَا وَٱسْمَعُوا۟ۗ وَلِلْكَٰفِرِينَ عَذَابٌ أَلِيمٌ ﴿١٠٤﴾

مَّا يَوَدُّ ٱلَّذِينَ كَفَرُوا۟ مِنْ أَهْلِ ٱلْكِتَٰبِ وَلَا ٱلْمُشْرِكِينَ أَن يُنَزَّلَ عَلَيْكُم مِّنْ خَيْرٍ مِّن رَّبِّكُمْۗ وَٱللَّهُ يَخْتَصُّ بِرَحْمَتِهِۦ مَن يَشَآءُۚ وَٱللَّهُ ذُو ٱلْفَضْلِ ٱلْعَظِيمِ ﴿١٠٥﴾

۞ مَا نَنسَخْ مِنْ ءَايَةٍ أَوْ نُنسِهَا نَأْتِ بِخَيْرٍ مِّنْهَآ أَوْ مِثْلِهَآ ۗ أَلَمْ تَعْلَمْ أَنَّ ٱللَّهَ عَلَىٰ كُلِّ شَىْءٍ قَدِيرٌ ﴿١٠٦﴾ أَلَمْ تَعْلَمْ أَنَّ ٱللَّهَ لَهُۥ مُلْكُ ٱلسَّمَٰوَٰتِ وَٱلْأَرْضِۗ وَمَا لَكُم مِّن دُونِ ٱللَّهِ مِن وَلِىٍّ وَلَا نَصِيرٍ ﴿١٠٧﴾ أَمْ تُرِيدُونَ أَن تَسْـَٔلُوا۟ رَسُولَكُمْ كَمَا سُئِلَ مُوسَىٰ مِن قَبْلُۗ وَمَن يَتَبَدَّلِ ٱلْكُفْرَ بِٱلْإِيمَٰنِ فَقَدْ ضَلَّ سَوَآءَ ٱلسَّبِيلِ ﴿١٠٨﴾ وَدَّ كَثِيرٌ مِّنْ أَهْلِ ٱلْكِتَٰبِ لَوْ يَرُدُّونَكُم مِّنۢ بَعْدِ إِيمَٰنِكُمْ كُفَّارًا حَسَدًا مِّنْ عِندِ أَنفُسِهِم مِّنۢ بَعْدِ مَا تَبَيَّنَ لَهُمُ ٱلْحَقُّۖ فَٱعْفُوا۟ وَٱصْفَحُوا۟ حَتَّىٰ يَأْتِىَ ٱللَّهُ بِأَمْرِهِۦٓۗ إِنَّ ٱللَّهَ عَلَىٰ كُلِّ شَىْءٍ قَدِيرٌ

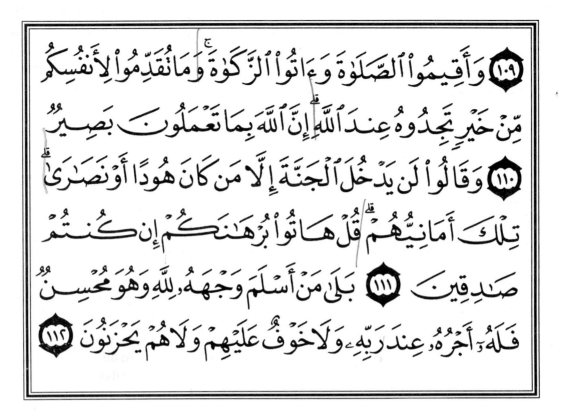

TRANSLATIONS

Section 13: 104-112 (A. Y. Ali)

Section 13: 104-112 (M. M. Pickthall)

104.   O you of Faith! Say not (to the Prophet) words of ambiguous import, but words of respect; and hearken (to him): to those without Faith is a grievous punishment.

105.   It is never the wish of those without faith among the People of the Book, nor of the Pagans, that anything good should come down to you from your Lord. But Allāh will choose for His special Mercy whom He will - for Allāh is Lord of grace abounding.

106.   None of Our revelations do We abrogate {repeal} or cause to be forgotten, but We substitute something better or similar: know you not that Allāh has power over all things?

107.   Know you not that to Allāh belongs the dominion {power} of the heavens and the earth? And besides Him you have neither patron nor helper.

108.   Would you question your Messenger as Moses was questioned of old? But whoever changes from Faith to Unbelief, has strayed without doubt from the even way.

104.   O you who believe, say not (unto the Prophet): "Listen to us" but say "Look upon us," and be you listeners. For disbelievers is a painful doom.

105.   Neither those who disbelieve among the People of the Scripture, nor the idolaters love that there should be sent down unto you any good thing from your Lord. But Allāh chooses for His mercy whom He will, and Allāh is of infinite bounty.

106.   Such of Our revelations as We abrogate {repeal} or cause to be forgotten, we bring (in place) one better or the like thereof. Knows you not that Allāh is Able to do all things?

107.   Knows you not that it is Allāh unto Whom belongs the sovereignty of the heavens and earth; and you have not, beside Allāh, any friend or helper?

108.   Or would you question your messenger as Moses was questioned aforetime? He who chooses disbelief instead of Faith; verily, he has gone astray from a plain road.

109. Quite a number of the People of the Book wish they could turn you (people) back to infidelity after you have believed. From selfish envy, after the truth has become manifest unto them: but forgive and overlook, till Allāh accomplishes His purpose: for Allāh has power over all things.

110. And be steadfast in prayer and regular in charity: and whatever good you send forth for your souls before you, you shall find it with Allāh: for Allāh sees well all that you do.

111. And they say: "None shall enter Paradise unless he be a Jew or a Christian." Those are their (vain) desires. Say: "Produce your proof if you are truthful."

112. Indeed - whoever submits his whole self to Allāh and is a doer of good - he will get his reward with his Lord; on such shall be no fear, nor shall they grieve.

109. Many of the People of the Scripture long {wish} to make you disbelievers after your belief, through envy on their own account, after the truth has become manifest unto them. Forgive and be indulgent {lenient} (toward them) until Allāh give command. Lo! Allāh is Able to do all things.

110. Establish worship, and pay the poor due; and whatever of good you send before (you) for your souls, you will find it with Allāh. Lo! Allāh is Seer of what you do.

111. And they say: None enters Paradise unless he be a Jew or a Christian. These are their own desires. Say: Bring your proof (of what you state) if you are truthful.

112. Indeed, but whosoever surrenders his purpose to Allāh while doing good, his reward is with his Lord; and there shall no fear come upon them neither shall they grieve.

EXPLANATION

104: The word disapproved is *Ra'ina*, which was used by Muslims to mean "Please look at us." The enemies twisted it to give insulting meaning. The general lesson is that we must guard ourselves from tricks using words of double meaning. Such words may sound complimentary, but they have a hidden insulting meaning..

105: {The People of the Book and the *Kuffār* were not ready to accept any teachings that would contradict their established beliefs. So, even though Muhammad's ﷺ message was far more perfect and thorough, they rejected it. They did not realize that despite their pretentions of having a special relationship with God, they had no control on His choice of the Prophet Muhammad ﷺ and his people to receive the mercy of His revelation. AG}

106: *'Ayāt*: translated as "revelations" is used for verses of the Qur'an, revelations of God, and for His other Signs in history or nature, or miracles. What is the meaning here? If we take it in a general sense, it means that God's Message from age to age remains the same, but many elements in its form may differ {as they were abrogated or added} according to the needs and demands of the time. Thus, the Message was the same, but its form was different as given to Moses, Jesus and Muhammad ﷺ. Some commentators apply it also to the *'Ayāt* of the Qur'ān. {There is detailed discussion and differing opinions on the question of *Naskh* of *'Ayāt* in *Ilm at-Tafsir* and must be followed there. AG}

107: {The disbelievers are warned and believers are assured that Allāh ﷻ is the Lord of Heaven and Earth, in full control of everything, and He is the True Friend of the righteous. AG}

108: Moses was constantly harassed with foolish and impertinent questions by his own people. We must not follow their example. Questions in religious matters are of utmost importance and should be asked respectfully for real instruction.
Sawa' as-Sabil, "Even way": the Arabic word *Sawa'* signifies smoothness as opposed to roughness: symmetry as opposed to crookedness. {Showing disobedience and disrespect to the Prophets leads one away from the straight path of faith to the crooked path of disbelief.

109: {The People of the Book opposed the children and followers of Ismā'il ﷺ simply out of jealousy. They should have naturally welcomed the *Kuffār* to turn to *Tawhid* and moral Islāmic life.

But they preferred for followers of the Prophet ﷺ to return to their old ways. So, the Prophet ﷺ is advised to ignore them and wait for the Judgment of Allāh ﷻ. AG}

'Afa (here translated "forgive") also means to forget, to obliterate from one's mind. *Safaha* (here translated "overlook") means to turn away from, to ignore, to treat a matter as if it did not affect one.

The word *'Amr* (translated here "to accomplish purpose") is a comprehensive term and includes (1) execution of a design; (2) an order or command; (3) a purpose or design. In many cases, some of these meanings run together.

110: {The Muslims must not be distracted by the idle talk of the People of the Book. They should continue to establish the *Ṣalāh*, pay the *Zak'ah* and continue to follow the commands of Allāh ﷻ. The reward they are going to receive from Allāh ﷻ is much beyond any of their expectations or services they had rendered. AG}

111-112: {The Jews and the Christians believe that the reward of the Hereafter is exclusively reserved for them. In fact, those who truly submit themselves to the Will of Allāh ﷻ and do righteous deeds will earn such rewards. AG}

Wajh (translated as "Self"): is a comprehensive Arabic word. It means (1) literally, "face", but it may imply; (2) countenance or favour; (3) glory or presence as applied to God, as in 2:115. (4) cause, sake; (5) nature, inner being, self. Here, I understand meaning 5; the whole inner self of the human.

The phrase, "On such shall be no fear, nor shall they grieve," comes in aptly in its own context many times. In this *Surah*, it occurs in 11, 38, 62, 112, 262, 274, and 277. It serves the same purpose as a refrain in a very well-arranged song.

IMPORTANT POINTS TO LEARN AND REFLECT UPON

- The believers must always use correct words, appropriate language and respectful speech.

- If the People of the Book try to turn Muslims away from the right path, Muslims must ask forgiveness and guidance for them while waiting for Allāh's ﷻ Judgment.

- The reward of Allāh ﷻ is for those who believe and do good deeds.

ARABIC GLOSSARY WORDS

بِسْمِ اللهِ الرَّحْمٰنِ الرَّحِيمِ

يَـٰٓأَيُّهَا الَّذِينَ اٰمَنُوا (104)O you who believe		الَّذِينَ كَفَرُوا	those who disbelieved
لَا تَقُولُوا	do not say	مِنْ أَهْلِ الْكِتٰبِ	among the People of the Book
رَاعِنَا	"pay attention to us"	وَلَا الْمُشْرِكِينَ	nor the Idolators
وَ قُولُوا	and (but) say	أَنْ يُنَزَّلَ عَلَيْكُمْ	that is sent down on you
اُنْظُرْنَا	"see us" ("please consider")	مِنْ خَيْرٍ	any good thing (i.e. revelation)
وَ اسْمَعُوا	and listen	مِنْ رَّبِّكُمْ	from your Lord
وَ لِلْكٰفِرِينَ	and for the disbelievers	وَ اللهُ يَخْتَصُّ	and Allah chooses (specifies)
عَذَابٌ أَلِيمٌ	(there is) painful punishment	بِرَحْمَتِهِ	for His Special Mercy
مَا يَوَدُّ (105)	Do not like (love)	مَنْ يَشَاءُ	whom He wants

وَ اللہُ	and Allah is	بِالْإِيمَانِ	for belief
ذُوالْفَضْلِ الْعَظِیم	(Lord) of Mighty Grace	فَقَدْ ضَلَّ	certainly has gone astray
(106) مَا نَنْسَخْ	We do not break	سَوَآءَ السَّبِیلِ	(from) the right way
مِنْ اٰیَةٍ	any sign(any command in the Book)	(109) وَدَّ كَثِیرٌ	Wished many
أَوْ نُنْسِهَا	nor let it be forgotten	مِنْ أَهْلِ الْكِتٰبِ	of the People of the Book
نَأْتِ	(but) We bring	لَوْ یَرُدُّوْنَكُمْ	that they could turn you back
بِخَیرٍ مِنْهَآ	better than it	مِنْ بَعْدِ إِیمَانِكُمْ	after you have become believers
أَوْ مِثْلِهَا	or similar to it	كُفَّارًا	(again into) disbelief
أَلَمْ تَعْلَمْ	did you not know	حَسَدًا	(out of) jealousy
أَنَّ اللہَ	that Allah (is)	مِنْ عِنْدِ أَنْفُسِهِمْ	within their (own) selves
عَلٰى كُلِّ شَیءٍ	on everything	مِنْ بَعْدِ	(even) after (the fact)
قَدِیرٌ	All Powerful	مَا تَبَیَّنَ	(that) became clear
(107) أَلَمْ تَعْلَمْ	Did you not know	لَهُمُ الْحَقُّ	to them the truth
أَنَّ اللہَ	that it is Allah	فَاعْفُوا	so pardon (them)
لَهُ مُلْكُ	to Him (belongs) kingdom	وَ اصْفَحُوا	and disregard
اَلسَّمٰوٰتِ	(of) the heavens	حَتّٰى یَأْتِیَ اللہُ	till Allah brings
وَ الْأَرْضِ	and the earth	بِأَمْرِهٖ	His command
وَمَا لَكُمْ	and there is not for you	إِنَّ اللہَ	indeed Allah is
مِنْ دُونِ اللہِ مِنْ	other than Allah	عَلٰى كُلِّ شَیءٍ	on everything
وَلِیٍّ	(neither) any protector	قَدِیرٌ	All-Powerful
وَّ لَا نَصِیرٍ	nor any helper	(110) وَ أَقِیمُوا الصَّلٰوةَ	And establish *Salah*
(108) أَمْ تُرِیدُونَ	Do you intend	وَ اٰتُوا الزَّكٰوةَ	and pay *Zakah*
أَنْ تَسْئَلُوا	that you ask (questions)	وَمَا تُقَدِّمُوا	and whatever you advance
رَسُولَكُمْ	from your messenger	لِأَنْفُسِكُمْ	for yourselves
كَمَا سُئِلَ مُوسٰى	as they asked Moses	مِنْ خَیرٍ	of good (deeds)
مِنْ قَبْلُ	earlier	تَجِدُوهُ	you shall find it
وَمَنْ یَّتَبَدَّلِ	and whoever exchanges	عِنْدَ اللہِ	with Allah
الْكُفْرَ	the disbelief	إِنَّ اللہَ	indeed Allah

بِمَا تَعْمَلُونَ	is of what you do	صٰدِقِينَ	truthful
بَصِيرٌ	All-Seeing	(112) بَلىٰ	Rather
(111) وَ قَالُوا	And they said	مَنْ أَسْلَمَ	one who surrenders
لَنْ يَّدْخُلَ	never (anyone) will enter	وَجْهَهُ لِلّٰهِ	himself (lit. his face) to Allah
اَلْجَنَّةَ	the Paradise	وَ هُوَ	and he is
إِلَّا مَنْ كَانَ	except one who is	مُحْسِنٌ	a doer of good
هُودًا أَوْ نَصٰرٰى	a Jew or a Christian	فَلَهُ أَجْرُهُ	so for him is his reward
تِلْكَ أَمَانِيُّهُمْ	these are their fancies	عِنْدَ رَبِّهِ	with his Lord
قُلْ هَاتُوا	say bring	وَ لَا خَوْفٌ	and neither there will be any fear
بُرْهَانَكُمْ	your proof	عَلَيْهِمْ	for them
إِنْ كُنْتُمْ	if you are	وَ لَا هُمْ يَحْزَنُونَ	nor they shall worry

SECTION -14-

Sūrah Al-Baqarah
2: 113-121

THE TEXT OF THE QUR'ĀN

بِسْمِ اللّٰهِ الرَّحْمٰنِ الرَّحِيمِ

وَقَالَتِ الْيَهُودُ لَيْسَتِ النَّصَارَى عَلَى شَيْءٍ وَقَالَتِ النَّصَارَى لَيْسَتِ الْيَهُودُ عَلَى شَيْءٍ وَهُمْ يَتْلُونَ الْكِتَابَ كَذَٰلِكَ قَالَ الَّذِينَ لَا يَعْلَمُونَ مِثْلَ قَوْلِهِمْ فَاللّٰهُ يَحْكُمُ بَيْنَهُمْ يَوْمَ الْقِيَامَةِ فِيمَا كَانُوا فِيهِ يَخْتَلِفُونَ ۝ وَمَنْ أَظْلَمُ مِمَّنْ مَنَعَ مَسَاجِدَ اللّٰهِ أَنْ يُذْكَرَ فِيهَا اسْمُهُ وَسَعَىٰ فِي خَرَابِهَا أُولَٰئِكَ مَا كَانَ لَهُمْ أَنْ يَدْخُلُوهَا إِلَّا خَائِفِينَ لَهُمْ فِي الدُّنْيَا خِزْيٌ وَلَهُمْ فِي الْآخِرَةِ عَذَابٌ عَظِيمٌ ۝ وَلِلّٰهِ الْمَشْرِقُ وَالْمَغْرِبُ فَأَيْنَمَا تُوَلُّوا فَثَمَّ وَجْهُ اللّٰهِ إِنَّ اللّٰهَ وَاسِعٌ عَلِيمٌ ۝ وَقَالُوا اتَّخَذَ اللّٰهُ وَلَدًا سُبْحَانَهُ بَلْ لَهُ مَا فِي السَّمَاوَاتِ وَالْأَرْضِ كُلٌّ لَهُ قَانِتُونَ ۝ بَدِيعُ السَّمَاوَاتِ وَالْأَرْضِ وَإِذَا قَضَىٰ أَمْرًا فَإِنَّمَا يَقُولُ لَهُ كُنْ فَيَكُونُ ۝ وَقَالَ الَّذِينَ لَا يَعْلَمُونَ لَوْلَا يُكَلِّمُنَا اللّٰهُ أَوْ تَأْتِينَا آيَةٌ كَذَٰلِكَ قَالَ الَّذِينَ مِنْ قَبْلِهِمْ مِثْلَ قَوْلِهِمْ تَشَابَهَتْ قُلُوبُهُمْ

قَدْ بَيَّنَّا ٱلْآيَٰتِ لِقَوْمٍ يُوقِنُونَ ۝ إِنَّآ أَرْسَلْنَٰكَ بِٱلْحَقِّ بَشِيرًا وَنَذِيرًا ۖ وَلَا تُسْـَٔلُ عَنْ أَصْحَٰبِ ٱلْجَحِيمِ ۝ وَلَن تَرْضَىٰ عَنكَ ٱلْيَهُودُ وَلَا ٱلنَّصَٰرَىٰ حَتَّىٰ تَتَّبِعَ مِلَّتَهُمْ ۗ قُلْ إِنَّ هُدَى ٱللَّهِ هُوَ ٱلْهُدَىٰ ۗ وَلَئِنِ ٱتَّبَعْتَ أَهْوَآءَهُم بَعْدَ ٱلَّذِى جَآءَكَ مِنَ ٱلْعِلْمِ ۙ مَا لَكَ مِنَ ٱللَّهِ مِن وَلِىٍّ وَلَا نَصِيرٍ ۝ ٱلَّذِينَ ءَاتَيْنَٰهُمُ ٱلْكِتَٰبَ يَتْلُونَهُۥ حَقَّ تِلَاوَتِهِۦٓ أُو۟لَٰٓئِكَ يُؤْمِنُونَ بِهِۦ ۗ وَمَن يَكْفُرْ بِهِۦ فَأُو۟لَٰٓئِكَ هُمُ ٱلْخَٰسِرُونَ ۝

TRANSLATIONS

Section 14: 113-121 (A. Y. Ali)

113. The Jews say: "The Christians have naught (to stand) upon"; and the Christians say: "The Jews have naught (to stand) upon." Yet, they (profess to) study the (same) Book. Like unto their word is what those say who know not; but Allāh will judge between them in their quarrel on the Day of Judgment.

114. And who is more unjust than he who forbids that in places for the worship of Allāh, His name should be celebrated? - Whose zeal is (in fact) to ruin them? It was not fitting that such should themselves enter them except in fear. For them, there is nothing but disgrace in this world, and in the world to come, an exceeding torment.

115. To Allāh belong the East and the West: whithersoever you turn, there is presence of Allāh. For Allāh is All-Pervading {al-Wāsi}, All-Knowing {al-ʿAlīm}.

116. They say: "Allah has begotten a

Section 14: 113-121 (M. M. Pickthall)

113. And the Jews say the Christians follow nothing (true), and the Christians say the Jews follow nothing (true); yet, both are readers of the Scripture. Even thus speak those who know not. Allāh will judge between them on the Day of Resurrection concerning that wherein they differ.

114. And who does greater wrong than he who forbids the approach to the sanctuaries {place of worship} of Allāh lest {last} His name should be mentioned therein, and strives for their ruin? As for such, it was never meant that they should enter them except in fear. Theirs in the world is ignominy and theirs in the Hereafter is an awful doom.

115. Unto Allāh belong the East and the West, and whithersoever you turn, there is Allāh's countenance. Lo! Allāh is All Embracing, All Knowing.

116. And they say: Allah has taken unto Him-son": Glory be to Him - indeed, to Him belongs all that is in the heavens and on earth: everything renders worship to Him.

117. To Him, is due the primal origin of the heavens and the earth: when He decrees {orders} a matter, He says to it: "Be," {*Kun*} and it is {*fa-yakūn*}.

118. Say those without knowledge: "Why speaks not Allāh unto us? Or why comes not unto us a sign?" So said the people before them words of similar import. Their hearts are alike. We have indeed made clear the Signs unto any people who hold firmly to Faith (in their hearts).

119. Verily, We have sent you in truth as a bearer of glad tidings {*Bashir*} and a warner {*Nadhīr*}: But of you no question shall be asked of the Companions of the Blazing Fire.

120. Never will the Jews or the Christians be satisfied with you unless you follow their form of religion. Say: "The Guidance of Allāh - that is the (only) Guidance," Were with you to follow their desires after the knowledge which has reached you, then would you find neither Protector nor Helper against Allāh.

121. Those to whom We have sent the Book study it as it should be studied: they are the ones that believe therein: those who reject Faith therein - the loss is their own.

self a Son. Be He glorified! Indeed, but whatsoever is in the heaven and the earth is His. All are subservient {inferior, obedient} unto Him.

117. The Originator of the heavens and the earth! When He decrees a thing, He says unto it only: Be! And it is.

118. And those who have no knowledge say: Why does not Allāh speak unto us, or some sign come unto us? Even thus, as they now speak, spoke those (who were) before them. Their hearts are all alike. We have made clear the revelations for people who are sure.

119. Lo! We have sent you (O Muḥammad) with the truth, a bringer of glad tidings and a warner. And you will not be asked about the owners of hell fire.

120. And the Jews will not be pleased with you, nor will the Christians, till you follow their creed. Say: Lo! The guidance of Allāh (Himself) is Guidance. And if you should follow their desires after the knowledge which has come unto you, then would you have from Allāh no protecting friend nor helper.

121. Those unto whom We have given the Scripture, who read it with the right reading, those believe in it. And whosoever disbelieves in it, those are they who are the losers.

EXPLANATION

113: It is a sure sign of ignorance and prejudice to deny the evident similarities in two books and to remain intolerant of the meaning which another person draws from it.

114: There were actually Pagans in Makkah who tried to shut out the Muslims from the Ka'bah, the universal place of Arab worship. If these Pagans had succeeded, they would only have caused violent divisions and destroyed the sanctity of the Ka'bah.

115: The word translated "presence" is *Wajh*, which literally means "face." - See note to 2:112 above.

116: It is an insult to the glory of God to say that God begets sons, like a human or an animal. The Christian doctrine is here emphatically repudiated. In a spiritual sense, we are all children of God. And all Creation celebrates His glory.

117: In case anyone should think that the heavens and the earth were themselves primeval or eternal, we are now told that they themselves are subjects of God's will and design. See 4:102, where the word *bada'a* is used as here for the creation of the heavens and the earth, and *khalaqa* is used for the creation of all things. In "things", we include abstract as well as material things. We see the abstract things and ideas actually growing before us. But that also is God's creation, to which we can apply the word *khalaqa*. The Qur'ān uses many words for the creation, each one has its own significance. The word "*amr*" (= command, direction, design) is a single thing, unrelated to time, "like the twinkling of an eye" (*Al-Qamar* 54:50). Another word to note in this connection is *ja'ala* (making) which seems to imply new shapes and forms. A further process with regard to the soul is described in the word *sawwa* - "bringing it to perfection" (*Ash-Shams* 91: 7). *Faṭara* (*Ash-Shura* 42:11) implies, like *bada'a*, the creating of a thing out of nothing and after no preexisting similitude, but perhaps *faṭara* implies the creation of primeval matter to which further processes have to be applied later. *Bada'a* (without the 'ain, *Ar-Rūm* 30:27), implies beginning the process of creation. Lastly, *bara'a* is creation implying liberation from pre-existing matter or circumstance, e.g., human body from clay (see *Al-Ḥashr* 59:24).

118:   {The non-believers did not pay attention to the teachings of the Qur'ān or the life and example of the Prophet ﷺ. Instead, they placed unreasonable demands before him. The signs of the revelation were clearly visible in both the Message and the Messenger for those who were prepared to see and accept the truth. AG.}

119:   {The Messenger was sent with the Message which brought good news to the righteous and informed of the evil consequences of disbelief. His mission is to deliver the message. He is not responsible for the actions of the disbelievers. AG.}

120:   {The Final Guidance of God has come. The truth of Islām was recognized by most of the Jews and the Christians. The disbelievers, however, not only rejected Islām, but would not be happy unless the Prophet ﷺ and the Muslims started following their beliefs. Such a case, however, was not possible. Hence, the Prophet ﷺ and the believers must not concern themselves with following the desires of the non-believers. They must do what God requires them to do. AG}

121:   {Among the People of the Book, there were some righteous people, who read their books to understand the truth. These were the first to believe in the final revelation. AG.}

IMPORTANT POINTS TO LEARN AND REFLECT UPON

- •   The Jews and the Christians differ with each other in the understanding of the revelation, even though its meanings are clear.

- •   To Allāh ﷻ belongs everything. He does not need a son like human beings do.

- •   We must study the Book of Allāh ﷻ as it must be studied, with understanding, respect, and intention to act upon it.

ARABIC GLOSSARY WORDS

بِسْمِ اللهِ الرَّحْمٰنِ الرَّحِيمِ

وَ قَالَتِ الْيَهُودُ (113) And the Jews said	عَلٰى شَىْءٍ	on anything
لَيْسَتِ النَّصْرٰى the Christian are not,	وَهُمْ	yet they
(do not stand)	يَتْلُونَ	recite
عَلٰى شَىْءٍ on anything	الْكِتٰبَ	the Book
وَقَالَتِ النَّصْرٰى and the Christians said	كَذٰلِكَ قَالَ	this is the way said
لَيْسَتِ الْيَهُودُ the Jews are not	الَّذِينَ	those who
(do not stand)	لَا يَعْلَمُونَ	do not know

مِثْلَ	similar	وَ لِلّٰهِ (115)	And to Allah (belong)
قَوْلِهِمْ	to their saying	اَلْمَشْرِقُ	the East
فَاللّٰهُ يَحْكُمُ	so Allah shall judge	وَالْمَغْرِبُ	and the West
بَيْنَهُمْ	between them	فَأَيْنَمَا	so wherever
يَوْمَ الْقِيٰمَةِ	(on) the Day of Resurrection	تُوَلُّوا	you turn
فِيْمَا	in (concerning) what	فَثَمَّ	there is
كَانُوْا فِيْهِ يَخْتَلِفُوْنَ	they were disputing in it	وَجْهُ	the Countenance
وَ مَنْ (114)	And who	اللّٰهِ	(of) Allah
أَظْلَمُ	is more unjust	إِنَّ اللّٰهَ	indeed Allah is
مِمَّنْ	than one who	وَاسِعٌ	All-Embracing
مَنَعَ	bars (forbids)	عَلِيْمٌ	All-Knowing
مَسٰجِدَ اللّٰهِ	places for worship of Allah	وَ قَالُوا (116)	And they said
أَنْ يُّذْكَرَ	from the remembrance	اتَّخَذَ اللّٰهُ	Allah has taken
	(lit. that is remembered)	وَلَدًا	a son
فِيْهَا	in it	سُبْحٰنَهُ	Glory be to Him
اسْمُهُ	of His name	بَلْ	nay
وَسَعٰى	and strives	لَهُ	to Him belongs
فِىْ خَرَابِهَا	for their ruin	مَا فِى	all that is in
أُولٰئِكَ	These people	اَلسَّمٰوٰتِ	the heavens
مَا كَانَ لَهُمْ	for them it was never meant	وَ الْأَرْضِ	and the earth
أَنْ يَّدْخُلُوْهَآ	that they would enter them	كُلٌّ	everyone is
إِلَّا خَآئِفِيْنَ	except fearing (Allah)	لَهُ	to Him
لَهُمْ	(there is) for them	قَانِتُوْنَ	(devoutly) obedient
فِى الدُّنْيَا	in this world	بَدِيْعُ (117)	Creator (of)
خِزْىٌ	a disgrace	اَلسَّمٰوٰتِ	the heavens
وَّ لَهُمْ	and (there is) for them	وَ الْأَرْضِ	and the earth
فِى الْآخِرَةِ	in the Hereafter	وَ إِذَا	and when
عَذَابٌ عَظِيْمٌ	a severe Punishment	قَضٰى	He decrees

أَمْرًا	a matter
فَإِنَّمَا يَقُولُ	so He only says
لَهُ	to it
كُنْ	"be"
فَيَكُونُ	so it becomes
وَ قَالَ (118)	And said
الَّذِينَ	those who
لَا يَعْلَمُونَ	do not know
لَوْ لَا	why does not
يُكَلِّمُنَا	speak to us (directly)
اللهُ	Allah
أَوْ	or
تَأْتِينَا	come to us
آيَةٌ	a sign
كَذَلِكَ	this is the way
قَالَ	spoke
الَّذِينَ مِنْ قَبْلِهِمْ	those who were before them
مِثْلَ	similar (to)
قَوْلِهِمْ	their saying
إِنَّا أَرْسَلْنَاكَ (119)	We sent you
بِالْحَقِّ	with the truth
بَشِيرًا	(as) a bearer of good tidings
وَّ نَذِيرًا	and a warner
وَّ لَا تُسْئَلُ	and you shall not be questioned
عَنْ	concerning
أَصْحَبِ	the Companions of
الْجَحِيمِ	Hell

وَ لَنْ تَرْضَى (120)	And will never be satisfied
عَنْكَ	with you
الْيَهُودُ	the Jews
وَ لَا النَّصْرَى	nor the Christians
حَتَّى	until
تَتَّبِعَ	you follow
مِلَّتَهُمْ	their religious path
قُلْ	say
إِنَّ هُدَى اللهِ	verily Guidance of Allah
هُوَ الْهُدَى	is the (real) guidance
وَ لَئِنِ	and surely if
اتَّبَعْتَ	you (O Prophet) follow
أَهْوَاءَهُمْ	their whims (fancies)
بَعْدَ الَّذِى	after that which
جَاءَكَ	has come to you
مِنَ الْعِلْمِ	from the knowledge
مَالَكَ مِنَ اللهِ	neither you shall have (to save) from (the Punishment of) Allah
مِنْ وَلِيٍّ	any protector
وَّ لَا نَصِيرٍ	(nor) any helper
الَّذِينَ (121)	Those whom
اتَيْنَهُمُ	We have given
الْكِتَبَ	the Book
يَتْلُونَهُ	they recite it
حَقَّ تِلَاوَتِهِ	a real recitation (or the way it should be recited)
أُولَئِكَ	those

يُؤْمِنُونَ بِهِ believe in it

وَمَنْ and who

يَكْفُرْ بِهِ disbelieves it

فَأُولَٰئِكَ هُمُ so those are the ones

الْخَاسِرُونَ who are the losers

SECTION -15-

Sūrah Al-Baqarah
2: 122-129

THE TEXT OF THE QUR'ĀN

بِسْمِ اللَّهِ الرَّحْمَٰنِ الرَّحِيمِ

يَٰبَنِىٓ إِسْرَٰٓءِيلَ اذْكُرُوا۟ نِعْمَتِىَ الَّتِىٓ أَنْعَمْتُ عَلَيْكُمْ وَأَنِّى فَضَّلْتُكُمْ عَلَى الْعَٰلَمِينَ ۝١٢٢ وَاتَّقُوا۟ يَوْمًا لَّا تَجْزِى نَفْسٌ عَن نَّفْسٍ شَيْـًٔا وَلَا يُقْبَلُ مِنْهَا عَدْلٌ وَلَا تَنفَعُهَا شَفَٰعَةٌ وَلَا هُمْ يُنصَرُونَ ۝١٢٣ وَإِذِ ابْتَلَىٰٓ إِبْرَٰهِۦمَ رَبُّهُۥ بِكَلِمَٰتٍ فَأَتَمَّهُنَّ قَالَ إِنِّى جَاعِلُكَ لِلنَّاسِ إِمَامًا قَالَ وَمِن ذُرِّيَّتِى قَالَ لَا يَنَالُ عَهْدِى الظَّٰلِمِينَ ۝١٢٤ وَإِذْ جَعَلْنَا الْبَيْتَ مَثَابَةً لِّلنَّاسِ وَأَمْنًا وَاتَّخِذُوا۟ مِن مَّقَامِ إِبْرَٰهِۦمَ مُصَلًّى وَعَهِدْنَآ إِلَىٰٓ إِبْرَٰهِۦمَ وَإِسْمَٰعِيلَ أَن طَهِّرَا بَيْتِىَ لِلطَّآئِفِينَ وَالْعَٰكِفِينَ وَالرُّكَّعِ السُّجُودِ ۝١٢٥ وَإِذْ قَالَ إِبْرَٰهِۦمُ رَبِّ اجْعَلْ هَٰذَا بَلَدًا ءَامِنًا وَارْزُقْ أَهْلَهُۥ مِنَ الثَّمَرَٰتِ مَنْ ءَامَنَ مِنْهُم بِاللَّهِ وَالْيَوْمِ الْءَاخِرِ قَالَ وَمَن كَفَرَ فَأُمَتِّعُهُۥ قَلِيلًا ثُمَّ أَضْطَرُّهُۥٓ إِلَىٰ عَذَابِ النَّارِ وَبِئْسَ الْمَصِيرُ ۝١٢٦ وَإِذْ يَرْفَعُ إِبْرَٰهِۦمُ الْقَوَاعِدَ مِنَ الْبَيْتِ وَإِسْمَٰعِيلُ رَبَّنَا تَقَبَّلْ مِنَّآ إِنَّكَ أَنتَ السَّمِيعُ الْعَلِيمُ ۝١٢٧ رَبَّنَا وَاجْعَلْنَا مُسْلِمَيْنِ

لَكَ وَمِن ذُرِّيَّتِنَا أُمَّةً مُّسْلِمَةً لَّكَ وَأَرِنَا مَنَاسِكَنَا وَتُبْ عَلَيْنَا إِنَّكَ أَنتَ التَّوَّابُ الرَّحِيمُ ۝ رَبَّنَا وَابْعَثْ فِيهِمْ رَسُولًا مِّنْهُمْ يَتْلُوا عَلَيْهِمْ ءَايَتِكَ وَيُعَلِّمُهُمُ الْكِتَبَ وَالْحِكْمَةَ وَيُزَكِّيهِمْ إِنَّكَ أَنتَ الْعَزِيزُ الْحَكِيمُ ۝

TRANSLATIONS

Section 15: 122-129 (A. Y. Ali)	Section 15: 122-129 (M. M. Pickthall)

122. O Children of Israel! Call to mind the special favor which I bestowed upon you, and that I preferred you to all others (for My Message).

123. Then guard yourselves against a Day when one soul shall not avail {benefit from} another. Nor shall compensation be accepted from her nor shall intercession profit her nor shall anyone be helped (from outside).

124. And remember that Abraham {Ibrāhīm} was tried by his Lord with certain Commands, which he fulfilled: He said: "I will make you an *Imām* to the nations." He pleaded: "And also *(Imams)* from my offspring!" He answered: "But my promise is not within the reach of evildoers."

125. Remember, We made the house a place of assembly for men and a place of safety; and take you the station of Abraham as a place of prayer; and We covenanted with Abraham and Ishmael (Ismā'il) that they should sanctify {purify} My House for those who compass it round or use it as a retreat, or bow or prostrate themselves (therein in prayer).

126. And remember Abraham said: "My Lord make this a City of Peace, and feed its People with fruits - such of them as believe in Allāh and the Last Day." He said: "(Yes), and such as reject Faith - for a while will I grant

122. O Children of Israel! Remember My favor wherewith I favored you, and how I preferred you to (all) creatures.

123. And guard (yourselves) against a day when no soul will naught avail another, nor will compensation be accepted from it, nor will intercession be of use to it; nor will they be helped.

124. And (remember) when his Lord tried Abraham {Ibrāhīm} with (His) commands, and he fulfilled them, He said: Lo! I have appointed you a leader for mankind. (Abraham) said: And of my offspring (will there be leaders)? He said: My Covenant includes not wrongdoers.

125. And when We made the House (at Makkah) a resort for mankind and a sanctuary, (saying): Take as your place of worship the place where Abraham stood (to pray). And We imposed a duty upon Abraham and Ishmael {Ismā'il}, (saying): Purify My house for those who go around and those who meditate therein and those who bow down and prostrate themselves (in worship).

126. And when Abraham prayed: My Lord! Make this a region of security and bestow upon its people fruits, such of them as believe in Allāh and the Last Day, He answered: As for him who disbelieves, I shall them their pleasure, but will soon drive them to the torment of Fire an evil destination (indeed)!"

127. And remember Abraham and Ishmael raised the foundations of the House (with this prayer): "Our Lord! {*Rabb*}! Accept (this service) from us: for you are the All-Hearing {*as-Sami'*}, the All-Knowing.

128. "Our Lord! Make of us Muslims, bowing to Your (Will), and of our progeny {offspring} a people Muslim, bowing to Your (Will) and show us our places for the celebration of (due) rites; and turn unto us (in mercy); for You are the Oft-Returning {*At-Tawwāb*} Most-Merciful {*Ar-Rahīm*}

129. "Our Lord! Send amongst them a Messenger of their own, who shall rehearse Your Signs to them and instruct them in Scripture {holy books} and Wisdom, and sanctify them; for You are the Exalted in Might the Wise."

leave him in contentment for a while, then I shall compel him to the doom of Fire - a hapless {unlucky} journey's end!

127. And when Abraham and Ishmael were raising the foundations of the House, Abraham prayed: Our Lord! Accept from us (this duty). Lo! You, only You, are the Hearer, the Knower.

128. Our Lord! And make us submissive unto You and of our seed {offspring} a nation submissive unto You, and show us our ways of worship, and relent toward us. Lo! You, only You, are the Relenting, the Merciful.

129. Our Lord! And raise up in their midst a Messenger from among them who shall recite unto them Your revelations, and shall instruct them in the Scripture and in wisdom and shall make them grow. Lo! You, only You, are the Mighty, Wise.

EXPLANATION

122-123: Verses 122-123 repeat verses 47-48 (except for a slight verbal variation.) After the argument about the favors to Israel, we now proceed to the argument in favor of the Arabs as succeeding to the spiritual inheritance of Ibrāhim.

124: *Kalimāt*, literally "words", used here in the sense of Allāh's Will or Decree or Purpose. In everything, Abraham fulfilled Allāh's wish, and he was promised the leadership of the world; he pleaded for his progeny, and his prayer was granted, except for the people who deviated from right path and proved themselves false.

125: The Ka'bah, the House of Allāh. Its foundation goes back by Arab tradition to Ibrāhim. Its fourfold character is referred to here. (1) It was the center to which all the Arab tribes gravitated; (2) It was sacred territory and was respected by friend and foe alike; (3) It was a place of prayer; (4) It was held pure and sacred for all purposes. Four rites are here enumerated: (1) The *Tawāf*, Compassing the sacred House; (2) Retiring to the place as a spiritual retreat; (3) The *Rukū'*, the posture of bending forward in prayer; and (4) *Sujūd*, the posture of prostration on the ground. The protection of the holy territory is for all, but special cleanliness and purity is required for the sake of the pilgrims.

126: Makkah is the city of Islām. It is also the City of Peace. The same root occurs in the latter part of the name Jerusalem, the Jewish City of Peace. When the day of Jerusalem passed (2:134 or 141), Makkah became the "New Jerusalem" - or rather the old and original "City of Peace" established by Ibrāhim - restored and made universal. The territory of Makkah is barren and rocky. A prayer for the prosperity of Makkah includes a prayer for the good things of material life as well as a spiritual allegory of great force and aptness.

127: {The example of Ibrāhim is presented here as both a practical man of action building Ka'bah and a devout believer praying to his Lord for the acceptance of his and his son's actions. AG}

128: {The concern of Ibrāhim is not only for his own actions, but extends to his descendents - both direct and spiritual. He wants to see them continue submitting to Allāh's commandments as true Muslims. AG}

129: {Ibrāhim's concern then goes beyond his progeny to humanity as he prays for a messenger from among them to teach them and purify them AG}. Paganism, star-worship, and planet-worship was first cleared out of Makkah by Ibrāhim ﷺ, who, along with his elder son Ismaʻil ﷺ, then built the Kaʼbah and established the rites and usages of the sacred city. Ibrāhim ﷺ then asked for a blessing on himself and his progeny generally, both the children of his eldest born, Ismaʻil ﷺ and his younger son, Isaac. With prophetic vision, he foresees that there will be corruption and backsliding in both branches of his family: Makkah will house 360 idols, and Jerusalem will become a harlot city (Ezekiel 16:15), a city of abomination. But the light of Islām will shine and reclaim the lost people in both branches and indeed in all the world. So, he prays for God's mercy, for a messenger in Makkah.

IMPORTANT POINTS TO LEARN AND REFLECT UPON

- Ibrāhim ﷺ was made the *Imām* (the leader) for all humanity after tests and trials.
- Ibrāhim ﷺ and son Ismaʻil ﷺ built Kaʼbah, a House for His worship.
- Ibrāhim ﷺ prayed for his son, his children and humanity; he asked Allāh ﷻ to send His final messenger to teach them the Truth.

ARABIC GLOSSARY WORDS

بِسْمِ اللهِ الرَّحْمٰنِ الرَّحِيمِ

يٰبَنِىٓ إِسْرَآءِيلَ	(122) O Children of Israel	شَفَاعَةٌ	an intercession
أُذْكُرُوا	remember	وَّ لَا هُمْ	nor they
نِعْمَتِىَ الَّتِىٓ	My blessing which	يُنْصَرُونَ	shall be helped
أَنْعَمْتُ	I bestowed	وَ إِذِ ابْتَلٰىٓ	(124) And when (Lord) tested
عَلَيْكُمْ	upon you	اِبْرٰهِيمَ رَبُّهُ	(his Lord) to Abraham
وَ أَنِّى فَضَّلْتُكُمْ	and I preferred you	بِكَلِمٰتٍ	with (certain) words
عَلَى الْعٰلَمِينَ	above all beings	فَأَتَمَّهُنَّ	so he fulfilled them
وَ اتَّقُوا	(123) And beware of	قَالَ	He said
يَوْمًا	a day	إِنِّى جَاعِلُكَ	"I am going to make you
لَّا تَجْزِى نَفْسٌ	((when) no one shall be of any avail)	لِلنَّاسِ إِمَامًا	a leader for the mankind"
		قَالَ	he said
عَنْ نَفْسٍ شَيْئًا	to anyone (else) at all	وَمِنْ ذُرِّيَّتِى	and of my progeny
وَّ لَا يُقْبَلُ	neither shall be accepted	قَالَ لَا يَنَالُ	He said " shall not reach
مِنْهَا	from one	عَهْدِى	My covenant
عَدْلٌ	a compensation	الظّٰلِمِينَ	the unjust people"
وَّ لَا تَنْفَعُهَا	(nor will be of any profit (for) it)	وَ إِذْ	(125) And call to mind
		جَعَلْنَا	when We made

اَلْبَيْتَ	the house
مَثَابَةً لِّلنَّاسِ	a meeting place for mankind
وَ أَمْنًا	and place of peace
وَ اتَّخِذُوا	and you take
مِنْ مَّقَامِ	the place
إِبْرَاهِيمَ	Of Abraham
مُصَلًّى	the place of worship
وَ عَهِدْنَآ	and we took a covenant
إِلَى إِبْرَاهِيمَ	from Abraham
وَ إِسْمَاعِيلَ	and Ishmail
أَنْ طَهِّرَا	that (they) purify
بَيْتِيَ	My House
لِلطَّائِفِينَ	for those who go round
وَ الْعَاكِفِينَ	and those who meditate
وَ الرُّكَّعِ	and bow
السُّجُودِ	make prostration
وَ إِذْ قَالَ	(126) And when said
إِبْرَاهِيمُ	Abraham
رَبِّ اجْعَلْ	O my Lord make
هٰذَا بَلَدًا	this city
اٰمِنًا	a place of safety
وَّ ارْزُقْ	and provide
أَهْلَهُ	its people
مِنَ الثَّمَرٰتِ	with the fruits
مَنْ اٰمَنَ	those who believed
مِنْهُمْ	among them
بِاللَّهِ	in Allah
وَ الْيَوْمِ الْاٰخِرِ	and the Last Day
قَالَ	He said

وَمَنْ كَفَرَ	and who disbelieved
فَأُمَتِّعُهُ	so I would let him enjoy
قَلِيلاً	a little
ثُمَّ	then
أَضْطَرُّهُ	I shall compel him
إِلَى عَذَابِ	to the punishment
النَّارِ	of the Fire
وَبِئْسَ الْمَصِيرُ	(and what a miserable resort (the Fire is!))
(127) وَ إِذْ يَرْفَعُ إِبْرَاهِيمُ	(And remember when Abraham was raising)
الْقَوَاعِدَ	the foundations
مِنَ الْبَيْتِ	of the House
وَ إِسْمَاعِيلُ	and Ishmael
رَبَّنَا تَقَبَّلْ	our Lord accept (this)
مِنَّا	from us
إِنَّكَ أَنْتَ	indeed, you
السَّمِيعُ	are All-Hearing
الْعَلِيمُ	All- Knowing
(128) رَبَّنَا وَاجْعَلْنَا	Our Lord and make us
مُسْلِمَيْنِ لَكَ	a community submissive to you
وَمِنْ ذُرِّيَّتِنَآ	and of our progeny
أُمَّةً مُسْلِمَةً لَّكَ	submissive (servants) to you
وَ أَرِنَا	and show us
مَنَاسِكَنَا	(our religious rites (ways of sacrifice and worship))
وَ تُبْ	and turn (in Mercy)
عَلَيْنَا	towards us
إِنَّكَ أَنْتَ	Indeed, You alone are

اَلتَّوَّابُ	Oft-Returning	اٰيٰتِكَ	Your signs
اَلرَّحِيمُ	Most Merciful	وَ يُعَلِّمُهُمْ	and shall teach them
رَبَّنَا (129)	Our Lord	اَلْكِتٰبَ	the Book
وَ ابْعَثْ فِيهِمْ	and raise up in their midst	وَ الْحِكْمَةَ	and the wisdom
رَسُولاً مِنْهُمْ	(a messenger from them (i.e. one of them))	وَ يُزَكِّيهِمْ	and shall purify them
يَتْلُوا	(who) shall recite	إِنَّكَ أَنْتَ	indeed You are
عَلَيْهِمْ	on (to) them	اَلْعَزِيزُ	All-mighty
		اَلْحَكِيمُ	All-Wise

SECTION -16-

Sūrah Al-Baqarah
2: 130-141

THE TEXT OF THE QUR'ĀN

بِسْمِ اللَّهِ الرَّحْمَٰنِ الرَّحِيمِ

وَمَن يَرْغَبُ عَن

مِّلَّةِ إِبْرَٰهِـۧمَ إِلَّا مَن سَفِهَ نَفْسَهُۥ ۚ وَلَقَدِ ٱصْطَفَيْنَٰهُ فِى ٱلدُّنْيَا ۖ

وَإِنَّهُۥ فِى ٱلْأَخِرَةِ لَمِنَ ٱلصَّٰلِحِينَ ﴿١٣٠﴾ إِذْ قَالَ لَهُۥ رَبُّهُۥٓ أَسْلِمْ ۖ

قَالَ أَسْلَمْتُ لِرَبِّ ٱلْعَٰلَمِينَ ﴿١٣١﴾ وَوَصَّىٰ بِهَآ إِبْرَٰهِـۧمُ بَنِيهِ

وَيَعْقُوبُ يَٰبَنِىَّ إِنَّ ٱللَّهَ ٱصْطَفَىٰ لَكُمُ ٱلدِّينَ فَلَا تَمُوتُنَّ إِلَّا

وَأَنتُم مُّسْلِمُونَ ﴿١٣٢﴾ أَمْ كُنتُمْ شُهَدَآءَ إِذْ حَضَرَ يَعْقُوبَ

ٱلْمَوْتُ إِذْ قَالَ لِبَنِيهِ مَا تَعْبُدُونَ مِنۢ بَعْدِى قَالُوا۟ نَعْبُدُ

إِلَٰهَكَ وَإِلَٰهَ ءَابَآئِكَ إِبْرَٰهِـۧمَ وَإِسْمَٰعِيلَ وَإِسْحَٰقَ إِلَٰهًا

وَٰحِدًا وَنَحْنُ لَهُۥ مُسْلِمُونَ ﴿١٣٣﴾ تِلْكَ أُمَّةٌ قَدْ خَلَتْ ۖ لَهَا

مَا كَسَبَتْ وَلَكُم مَّا كَسَبْتُمْ ۖ وَلَا تُسْـَٔلُونَ عَمَّا كَانُوا۟ يَعْمَلُونَ ﴿١٣٤﴾

وَقَالُوا۟ كُونُوا۟ هُودًا أَوْ نَصَٰرَىٰ تَهْتَدُوا۟ ۗ قُلْ بَلْ مِلَّةَ إِبْرَٰهِـۧمَ

حَنِيفًا ۖ وَمَا كَانَ مِنَ ٱلْمُشْرِكِينَ ﴿١٣٥﴾ قُولُوٓا۟ ءَامَنَّا بِٱللَّهِ وَمَآ

أُنزِلَ إِلَيْنَا وَمَآ أُنزِلَ إِلَىٰٓ إِبْرَٰهِـۧمَ وَإِسْمَٰعِيلَ وَإِسْحَٰقَ وَيَعْقُوبَ

وَٱلۡأَسۡبَاطِ وَمَآ أُوتِيَ مُوسَىٰ وَعِيسَىٰ وَمَآ أُوتِيَ ٱلنَّبِيُّونَ مِن رَّبِّهِمۡ لَا نُفَرِّقُ بَيۡنَ أَحَدٖ مِّنۡهُمۡ وَنَحۡنُ لَهُۥ مُسۡلِمُونَ ۝١٣٦ فَإِنۡ ءَامَنُواْ بِمِثۡلِ مَآ ءَامَنتُم بِهِۦ فَقَدِ ٱهۡتَدَواْۖ وَّإِن تَوَلَّوۡاْ فَإِنَّمَا هُمۡ فِي شِقَاقٖۖ فَسَيَكۡفِيكَهُمُ ٱللَّهُۚ وَهُوَ ٱلسَّمِيعُ ٱلۡعَلِيمُ ۝١٣٧ صِبۡغَةَ ٱللَّهِۖ وَمَنۡ أَحۡسَنُ مِنَ ٱللَّهِ صِبۡغَةٗۖ وَنَحۡنُ لَهُۥ عَٰبِدُونَ ۝١٣٨ قُلۡ أَتُحَآجُّونَنَا فِي ٱللَّهِ وَهُوَ رَبُّنَا وَرَبُّكُمۡ وَلَنَآ أَعۡمَٰلُنَا وَلَكُمۡ أَعۡمَٰلُكُمۡ وَنَحۡنُ لَهُۥ مُخۡلِصُونَ ۝١٣٩ أَمۡ تَقُولُونَ إِنَّ إِبۡرَٰهِـۧمَ وَإِسۡمَٰعِيلَ وَإِسۡحَٰقَ وَيَعۡقُوبَ وَٱلۡأَسۡبَاطَ كَانُواْ هُودًا أَوۡ نَصَٰرَىٰۗ قُلۡ ءَأَنتُمۡ أَعۡلَمُ أَمِ ٱللَّهُۗ وَمَنۡ أَظۡلَمُ مِمَّن كَتَمَ شَهَٰدَةً عِندَهُۥ مِنَ ٱللَّهِۗ وَمَا ٱللَّهُ بِغَٰفِلٍ عَمَّا تَعۡمَلُونَ ۝١٤٠ تِلۡكَ أُمَّةٞ قَدۡ خَلَتۡۖ لَهَا مَا كَسَبَتۡ وَلَكُم مَّا كَسَبۡتُمۡۖ وَلَا تُسۡـَٔلُونَ عَمَّا كَانُواْ يَعۡمَلُونَ ۝١٤١

TRANSLATIONS

Section 16: 130-141 (A. Y. Ali)

Section 16: 130-141 (M. M. Pickthall)

130.   And who turns away from the religion of Abraham but such as debase their souls with folly? Him We chose and rendered pure in this world: and he will be in the Hereafter in the ranks of the Righteous.

131.   Behold! His Lord said to him: "Bow (your will to me):" He said: "I bow

130.   And who forsakes the religion of Abraham but him who befools himself? Verily, We chose him in the world, and lo! In the Hereafter he is among the righteous.

131.   When his Lord said unto him: Surrender! He said: I have surrendered to the Lord of the

(my will) to **the** Lord and Cherisher of the universe."

132. And this was the legacy that Abraham left to his sons, and so did Jacob {Ya'qūb}; "O my sons! Allāh has chosen the Faith for you; then die not except in the Faith of Islam."

133. Were you witnesses when death appeared before Jacob? Behold, he said to his sons: "What will you worship after me?" They said: "We shall worship your God and the God of your fathers, of Abraham, Ishmael and Isaac- the one (true) Allāh to Him we bow (in Islam)."

134. That was a People that has passed away. They shall reap the fruit of what they did, and you of what you do! Of their merits, there is no question in your case!

135. They say: "Become Jews or Christians if you would be guided (to salvation)." Say you: "Nay! (I would rather) the Religion of Abraham, the True, and he joined not gods with Allāh."

136. Say you: "We believe in Allāh, and the revelation given to us, and to Abraham, Ishmael, Isaac, Jacob, and the Tribes, and that given to Moses and Jesus, and that given to (all) Prophets from their Lord: we make no difference between one and another of them: and we bow to Allāh (in Islam)."

137. So if they believe as you believe they are indeed on the right path; but if they turn back, it is they who are in schism {split, division}; but Allāh will suffice you as against them, and He is the All-Hearing *{As-Samī'}* the All- Knowing *{Al-'Alīm}*

138. (Our religion is) the Baptism of Allāh; and who can baptize better than Allāh? And it is He whom we worship.

139. Say: Will you dispute with us about Allāh, seeing that He is our Lord and your Lord; that we are responsible for our doings, and you for yours; and that we are sincere (in our faith) in Him?

140. Or do you say that Abraham,

Worlds.

132. The same did Abraham enjoin upon his sons, and also Jacob {Ya'qūb}, (saying): O my sons! Lo! Allāh has chosen for you the (true) religion; therefore, die not but as men who have surrendered (unto Him).

133. Or were you present when death came to Jacob, when he said unto his sons: What will you worship after me? They said: We shall worship your God, the God of your fathers, Abraham and Ishmael and Isaac, One God, and unto Him we have surrendered.

134. Those are a people who have passed away. Theirs is that which they earned, and yours is that which you earn. And you will not be asked of what they used to do.

135. And they say: Be Jews or Christians, then you will be rightly guided. Say (unto them, O Muḥammad): Nay, but (we follow) the religion of Abraham, the upright, and he was not of the idolaters.

136. Say (O Muslims): We believe in Allah and that which is revealed unto us and that which was revealed unto Abraham, and Ishmael, and Isaac, and Jacob, and the tribes, and that which Moses and Jesus received, and that which the Prophets received from their Lord. We make no distinction between any of them, and unto Him we have surrendered.

137. And if they believe in the like of that which you believe, then are they rightly guided. But if they turn away, then are they in schism {split, division}, and Allāh will suffice you (for defense) against them. He is the Hearer, the Knower.

138. (We take our) color from Allāh, and who is better than Allāh at coloring. We are His worshippers.

139. Say (unto the People of the Scripture): Dispute you with us concerning Allāh when He is our Lord and your Lord? Ours are our works, and yours your works. We look to Him alone.

140. Or say you that Abraham, and

Ishmael, Isaac, Jacob and the Tribes were Jews or Christians? Say: Do you know better than Allāh? Ah! who is more unjust than those who conceal the testimony {evidence} they have from Allāh? But Allāh is not unmindful of what you do!

141. That was a people that has passed away. They shall reap the fruit of what they did, and you of what you do! Of their merits there is no question in your case: (community), justly balanced.

Ishmael, and Isaac, and Jacob, and the tribes were Jews or Christians? Say: Do you know best, or does Allāh? And who is more unjust than he who hides a testimony {evidence} which he has received from Allāh? Allāh is not unaware of what you do.

141. Those are a people who have passed away; theirs is that which they earned and yours that which you earn. And you will not be asked of what they used to do.

EXPLANATION

130: Ibrāhim 🕮 was chosen (*Iṣṭafā*) after many tests and trials because of his faith and purity. The root word *Iṣṭafā* means chosen; chosen because of purity. It is the same root from which *Muṣṭafa*, from which one of the titles of Prophet Muḥammad 🕮, is derived.

131: {Ibrāhim 🕮 was chosen for his unflinching, unwavering faith in Allāh 🕮. AG}

132: {The religion of Islām has been chosen by Allāh 🕮 for all people and for all time to come. One must live and die for this Faith to be worthy of Divine Grace and Favors}.

133: c. 131. The concept of Allāh 🕮 in the Jewish mind got narrowed down to that of a tribal god. But they are reminded that their ancestors believed in the principle of Islām- the worship of the One True and Universal God. {Note, the true concern of both Ibrāhim 🕮 and his son and grandson for the continuity of the true teachings of Islām through their generations. They are not asking God to grant their children worldly benefits, but rather a true faith. AG} "Fathers" means ancestors.

134: I have made a free paraphrase of what would read literally: "Ye shall not be asked about what they used to do." On the Day of Judgment, each soul will have to answer for its own deeds: it cannot claim merit from others, nor be answerable for the crimes or sins of others. The doctrine of personal responsibility is a cardinal feature of Islām.

135: Ibrāhim 🕮 was a *Hanīf*, inclined to right opinion, firm in faith, well-balanced and true.

136: {Muslims believe in all the messengers and do not prefer one over the other AG}.

137: We Muslims are thus in the true line of those who follow the one and indivisible Message of the One God, wherever delivered. If others narrow it or corrupt it, it is they who have left the faith and created a division or schism.

138: *Sibghat*: baptism; the root-meaning implies a dye or color; used by Arab Christians for the baptismal water. Our higher baptism is acceptance of Islām, by which we take on a color of true faith and in accepting Divine Revelation, we absorb the goodness that Allāh 🕮 wants for us.

139-140: The alternative is with the question. Do you dispute with us although we worship the same God as you and claim that ours is the same religion as that of your ancestors? Or do you really assert that Abraham and his son, and his sons' sons, who founded the tribes long before Moses, followed your Jewish religion as you know it? History, of course, proves that claim to be absurd. If the Christians claim that these patriarchs followed the teaching of Jesus, the claim is still more absurd - except in the Islām is sense that God's teaching is One in all ages.

141: Verse 134 began a certain argument, which is now rounded off in the same words in this verse. The argument is that it is wrong to claim a monopoly on God's Message. It is the same for all peoples and in all ages. If it undergoes local variations or changes according to times and seasons, those variations pass away. This leads to the argument in the remainder of the *Sūrah* that with the renewal of the Message and the birth of a new People, the Muslim `Ummah a new symbolism and new ordinances become appropriate, and they are now expounded.

IMPORTANT POINTS TO LEARN AND REFLECT UPON

- The true way of Ibrāhīm ☘ is Islām, and only those with impure souls turn away from his path.

- We Muslims believe in the message of all the prophets, and make no distinctions among them.

- Every individual and people is responsible before Allāh ﷻ of what they do.

ARABIC GLOSSARY WORDS

بِسْمِ اللهِ الرَّحْمٰنِ الرَّحِيمِ

وَ مَنْ	(130) And who	وَوَصّٰى بِهَآ	(132) And commissioned with it, (as legacy)
يَّرْغَبُ	shall turn away	إِبْرٰهِيمُ	Abraham
عَنْ	from	بَنِيهِ	on his sons
مِلَّةِ إِبْرٰهِيمَ	Abraham's religious path	وَ يَعْقُوبُ	and Jacob (did the same)
إِلَّا	except	يٰبَنِيَّ	On my sons
مَنْ سَفِهَ	one who fools	إِنَّ اللهَ	indeed Allah
نَفْسَهُ	himself	اصْطَفٰى	chose
وَ لَقَدِ	and definitely	لَكُمُ	for you
اصْطَفَيْنٰهُ	We had chosen him	الدِّينَ	the Religion (Islam)
فِى الدُّنْيَا	in this world	فَلَا تَمُوتُنَّ	so you must not die
وَ إِنَّهُ	and indeed he is	إِلَّا	except
فِى الْاٰخِرَةِ	in the Hereafter	وَأَنْتُمْ	that you are
لَمِنَ الصّٰلِحِينَ	(surely, among the righteous ones)	مُسْلِمُونَ	muslim, (i.e. submissive to Allah)
إِذْ قَالَ	(131) Remember when said	أَمْ كُنْتُمْ	(133) Were you
لَهُ	to him	شُهَدَآءَ	witness
رَبُّهُ	his Lord	إِذْ حَضَرَ يَعْقُوبَ	when came to Jacob
أَسْلِمْ	"submit"	الْمَوْتُ	the death
قَالَ أَسْلَمْتُ	he said "I submitted"	إِذْ قَالَ	when he said
لِرَبِّ	to the Lord (of)	لِبَنِيهِ	to his sons
الْعٰلَمِينَ	all the worlds"		

مَا تَعْبُدُونَ	what you shall worship	مِنَ الْمُشْرِكِينَ	of those who are Mushrik
مِنْ بَعْدِى	after me?	(136) قُولُوا	Say
قَالُوا	they said	اٰمَنَّا بِاللهِ	we believe in Allah
نَعْبُدُ	we shall worship	وَمَا أُنْزِلَ	and what is sent down
إِلٰهَكَ	your deity	إِلَيْنَا	to us
وَإِلٰهَ اٰبَائِكَ	and the deity of your fathers	وَمَا أُنْزِلَ	and what was sent down
إِبْرٰهِيمَ	Abraham	إِلٰى إِبْرٰهِيمَ	to Abraham
وَ إِسْمٰعِيلَ	and Ishmael	وَ إِسْمٰعِيلَ	and Ishmael
وَ إِسْحٰقَ	and Isaac	وَ إِسْحٰقَ	and Isaac
إِلٰهًا وَّاحِدًا	(the only) One Deity	وَ يَعْقُوبَ	and Jacob
وَّ نَحْنُ	and we are	وَالْأَسْبَاطَ	and the descendents
لَهُ, مُسْلِمُونَ	*Muslims* i.e. submissive to Him	وَمَا أُوتِيَ	and what was given to
(134) تِلْكَ أُمَّةٌ	That is a community	مُوسٰى وَ عِيسٰى	Moses and Jesus
قَدْ خَلَتْ	(which) has passed away	وَمَا أُوتِيَ	and what were given
لَهَا	for it (there is)	النَّبِيُّونَ	the prophets
مَا كَسَبَتْ	whatever it earned	مِنْ رَبِّهِمْ	from their Lord
وَلَكُمْ	and for you	لَا نُفَرِّقُ	we make no discrimination
مَا كَسَبْتُمْ	whatever you earned	بَيْنَ أَحَدٍ مِنْهُمْ	against (between) any of them
وَ لَا تُسْئَلُونَ	and you shall not be questioned	وَ نَحْنُ لَهُ	and we are to Him
عَمَّا	concerning what	مُسْلِمُونَ	submissive servants.
كَانُوا يَعْمَلُونَ	they had been doing	(137) فَإِنْ اٰمَنُوا	So if they believed
(135) وَ قَالُوا	And they said	بِمِثْلِ	the way (lit. like that which)
كُونُوا هُودًا	Become Jews	مَا اٰمَنْتُمْ بِهِ	you believed in it
أَوْ نَصٰرٰى	or Christians	فَقَدِ اهْتَدَوْا	then they have become guided
تَهْتَدُوا	you will be guided	وَ إِنْ تَوَلَّوْا	and if they turned away
قُلْ بَلْ	say rather	فَإِنَّمَا هُمْ	then(this) only (means) that they
مِلَّةَ إِبْرٰهِيمَ	(follow) path (of) Abraham	فِى شِقَاقٍ	are in severe opposition
حَنِيفًا	with loyalty (to God)	فَسَيَكْفِيكَهُمُ اللهُ	so will suffice you Allah
وَ مَا كَانَ	and he was not	وَ هُوَ	and He is

السَّمِيعُ الْعَلِيمُ All-Hearing, All-Knowing

كَانُوا هُودًا were Jews

(138)(Take)Allah's color صِبْغَةَ الله

أَوْ نَصَارَى or Christians

وَ مَنْ أَحْسَنُ and who is better

قُلْ ءَأَنْتُمْ say do you

مِنَ الله than Allah

أَعْلَمُ know more

صِبْغَةً (in) color?

أَمِ اللَّهُ or Allah?

وَّ نَحْنُ لَهُ and we are (only) His

وَ مَنْ أَظْلَمُ and who would be more unjust

عَابِدُونَ servants

مِمَّنْ كَتَمَ شَهَادَةً than one who hides a testimony

(139) Say "do you قُلْ أَتُحَاجُّونَنَا

عِندَهُ مِنَ الله he has from Allah

argue with us?"

وَ مَا اللَّهُ بِغَافِلٍ and Allah is not unaware

فِى الله concerning Allah

عَمَّا تَعْمَلُونَ of what you people do

وَ هُوَ رَبُّنَا and He is our Lord

(141) That community تِلْكَ أُمَّةٌ

وَرَبُّكُمْ and your Lord

قَدْ خَلَتْ has passed away

وَ لَنَا أَعْمَالُنَا and for us our deeds

لَهَا for it (there awaits)

وَلَكُمْ أَعْمَالُكُمْ and for you your deeds

مَا كَسَبَتْ whatever it earned

وَ نَحْنُ لَهُ and we are to him

وَلَكُمْ and (there awaits) for you

مُخْلِصُونَ sincere (purely his servant)

مَّا كَسَبْتُمْ whatever you earned

(140) Or do you say? أَمْ تَقُولُونَ

وَ لَا تُسْئَلُونَ and you shall not be questioned

إِنَّ إِبْرَاهِيمَ وَ إِسْمَاعِيلَ that Abraham and Ishmael

عَمَّا concerning what

وَ إِسْحَاقَ وَ يَعْقُوبَ and Isaac and Jacob

كَانُوا يَعْمَلُونَ they had been doing

وَ الْأَسْبَاطَ and the (the tribes)

APPENDIX 1.
ḤURŪF AL-MUQAṬṬA'ĀT: The Abbreviated Letters

Certain *Sūrahs* have certain initials prefixed to them, which are called the "Abbreviated letters," or "Separated Letters". A number of conjectures have been made as to their meaning. Opinions are divided as to the exact meaning of each particular letter or combination of letters, and it is agreed that Allāh ﷻ knows their exact meaning.

Their presence is not inconsistent with the character of the Qur'ān as a "plain book." The book of nature is also a plain book, but how few can fully understand it? Everyone can get out of the Qur'ān plain guidance for his life according to his capacity for spiritual understanding. As his capacity grows, so will his understanding grow. The whole Book is a record for all time. It must necessarily contain truths that only gradually unfold themselves to humanity. This is not a mystery of the same class as "mysteries" by which we are asked to believe against the dictates or reason.

There are 29 letters in the Arabic alphabet (counting *hamza* and *alif* as two letters), and there are 29 *Sūrahs* which have abbreviated letters prefixed to them. One of these *Sūrahs* (S. 42.) has two sets of abbreviated letters, but we need not count this *Sūrah* twice. If we take the half of the alphabet, omitting the fraction, we get 14, and this is the number of letters which actually occur in the *Muqaṭṭa'āt*.

The 14 letters, which occur in various combinations, are:

Alif	أ	Qāf	ق
Ḥā'	ح	kāf	ك
Rā'	ر	Lām	ل
Sīn	س	Mīm	م
Ṣād	ص	Nūn	ن
Ṭā'	ط	Hā'	ه
'Ayn	ع	Yā'	ى

The science of the phonetics tells us that our vocal sounds arise from the expulsion of the air from the lungs, and the sounds are determined by the way in which the breath passes through the various organs of speech. Everyone of these kinds of sounds is represented in these letters.

An arithmetical analysis of the *Sūrahs* starting with *Al-Muqaṭṭa'āt* brings certain facts into prominence, but we do not know how far they have a bearing on the inner meaning of the *Muqaṭṭa'āt*.

There are also some suggestions to logically look for a common factor in the *Sūrahs* bearing the same initials. We see in all that cases where the abbreviated letters occur, there is some mention of the Qur'ān or the Book. However, we cannot speak about other aspects with certainty.

There is no doubt that these *Ḥurūf al-Muqaṭṭa'āt* are part of the Qur'ān and their reading brings *barakah* but their meanings have been left as a mystery by Allāh ﷻ, and His messenger ﷺ, and our faith requires to accept them as they are.

(Based upon the translation of `Abidullāh Yūsuf `Alī`)

IQRA'
TRANSLITERATION CHART

q	ق	*	z	ز	,	أء *
k	ك		s	س	b	ب
l	ل		sh	ش	t	ت
m	م		ṣ	ص	* th	ث *
n	ن		ḍ	ض	* j	ج
h	ه		ṭ	ط	* ḥ	ح *
w	و		ẓ	ظ	* kh	خ *
y	ي		'	ع	* d	د *
			gh	غ	* dh	ذ *
			f	ف		r	ر

SHORT VOWELS	LONG VOWELS	DIPHTHONGS
a \ ﹷ	ā \ ﺎ	aw \ ﹷوْ
u \ ﹹ	ū \ ﹹو	ai \ ﹷيْ
i \ ﹻ	ī \ ﹻي	

Such as: *kataba* كَتَبَ	Such as: *Kitāb* كِتَاب	Such as: *Lawh* لَوْح
Such as: *Qul* قُلْ	Such as: *Mamnūn* مَمْنُون	Such as: *'Ain* عَيْن
Such as: *Ni'mah* نِعْمَة	Such as: *Dīn* دين	

* Special attention should be given to the symbols marked with stars for they have no equivalent in the English sounds.

Note : Letters in parenthesis (a),(i),(u) appear in writing but are not pronounced.

ISLAMIC INVOCATIONS:

Rasūlullāh, *Ṣalla Allahu 'alaihi wa Sallam* (صَلَّى ٱللَّهُ عَلَيْهِ وَسَلَّم), and the Qur'ān teaches us to glorify Allāh ﷻ when we mention His Name and to invoke His Blessings when we mention the names of His Angels, Messengers, the *Ṣaḥābah* and the Pious Ancestors.

When we mention the Name of Allāh we must say: *Subḥāna-hū Wa-Ta'ālā* (سُبْحَانَهُ وَتَعَالَى), Glorified is He and High. In this book we write ﷻ to remind ourselves to glorify Allāh.

When we mention the name of Rasūlullāh ﷺ we must say: *Ṣalla Allāhu 'alai-hi wa-Sallam,* (صَلَّى ٱللَّهُ عَلَيْهِ وَسَلَّم), May Allāh's Blessings and Peace be upon him.
We write ﷺ to remind ourselves to invoke Allāh's Blessings on Rasūlullāh.

When we mention the name of an angel or a prophet we must say: *Alai-hi-(a)s-Salām* (عَلَيْهِ ٱلسَّلَام), Upon him be peace.
We write ؑ to remind ourselves to invoke Allāh's Peace upon him.

When we hear the name of the *Ṣaḥābah* we must say:
For a *Ṣaḥābī, Raḍiya-(A)llāhu Ta'ālā 'an-hu* (رَضِيَ ٱللَّهُ تَعَالَى عَنْهُ), May Allāh be pleased with him.
We write ؓ to remind ourselves to invoke Allah's pleasure on them.

For more than two, *Raḍiya-(A)llāhu Ta'ālā 'an-hum,* (رَضِيَ ٱللَّهُ تَعَالَى عَنْهُم), May Allāh be pleased with them.
We write ؓ to remind ourselves to invoke Allah's pleasure on them.

For a *Ṣaḥābiyyah, Raḍiya-(A)llāhu Ta'ālā 'an-hā* (رَضِيَ ٱللَّهُ تَعَالَى عَنْهَا), May Allāh be pleased with her.
We write ؓ to remind ourselves to invoke Allah's pleasure on her.

For two of them, *Raḍiya-(A)llāhu Ta'ālā 'an-humā* (رَضِيَ ٱللَّهُ تَعَالَى عَنْهُمَا), May Allāh be pleased with both of them.
We write ؓ to remind ourselves to invoke Allah's pleasure on them.

When we hear the name of the Pious Ancestor *(As-Salaf aṣ-Ṣāliḥ)* we must say:
For a man, *Rahmatu-(A)llāh 'alai-hi* (رَحْمَةُ ٱللَّهِ عَلَيْهِ), May Allāh's Mercy be upon him.
For a woman, *Rahmatu-(A)llāh 'alai-hā* (رَحْمَةُ ٱللَّهِ عَلَيْهَا), May Allāh's Mercy be with her.

INTRODUCING THE AUTHOR

Dr. Abidullah Ghazi, Executive Director of IQRA' International, and his wife, Dr. Tasneema Ghazi, Director of Curriculum, are co–founders of IQRA' International Educational Foundation (a non–profit Islamic educational trust) and Chief Editors of its educational program. They have combined their talents and expertise and dedicated their lives to produce a <u>Comprehensive Program of Islamic Studies</u> for our children and youth and to develop IQRA' into a major center of research and development for Islamic Studies, specializing in Islamic education.

Abidullah Ghazi, M. A. (Alig), M. Sc. Econ. (LSE London), Ph. D. (Harvard)

Dr. Abidullah Ghazi, a specialist in Islamic Studies and Comparative Religion, belongs to a prominent family of the Ulama' of India. His family has been active in the field of Islamic education, *dawah*, and struggle for freedom. Dr. Ghazi's early education was carried in traditional *Madaris*. He later studied at Muslim University, Aligarh, The London School of Economics, and Harvard University. He has taught at the Universities of Jamia Millia Islamia, Delhi, London, Harvard, San Diego, Minnesota, Northwestern, Governors State and King Abdul Aziz, Jeddah. He is a consultant for the development of the program of Islamic Studies in various schools and universities. He is a well–known community worker, speaker, writer and poet.